Bricks and Blondie

WE NAILED IT!
THE BLUEPRINT FOR REAL ESTATE AND RELATIONSHIPS

DOUGLAS PARSON JR. *and* **ATIYA PARSON, PHD**

©Copyright 2023 Douglas Parson, Jr. and Atiya Parson

All rights reserved. This book is protected under the copyright laws of the United States of America.

ISBN-13: 978-1-954609-55-6

No portion of this book may be reproduced, distributed, or transmitted in any form, including photocopying, recording, or other electronic or mechanical methods, without the written permission of the publisher, except in the case of brief quotations embodied in reviews and certain other non-commercial uses permitted by copyright law. Permission granted on request.

For information regarding special discounts for bulk purchases, please contact the publisher: LaBoo Publishing Enterprise, LLC
staff@laboopublishing.com
www.laboopublishing.com

Introduction 1

Chapter 1: The Blueprint—The Beginning:
The Evolution of Bricks and Blondie 7

Chapter 2: Time to Build:
Break Ground with Us!. 21

Chapter 3: A Strong Foundation:
You Can't Build Without One 31

Chapter 4: Framing Your House and
Marriage to Stand the Test of Time. 41

Chapter 5: Weathering the Bad Times…Your Roof!. 47

Chapter 6: Materials: Show What You are Made Of! 55

Chapter 7: Wiring…What kind of energy is
brought into the marriage?. 63

Chapter 8: Systems in place! 69

Chapter 9: I'm gonna blow this house down…
     let us pray! 75

Chapter 10: We Nailed it! 83

Epilogue 89

About The Authors. 105

Dedication

To our mothers, Elizabeth Fouce and Patricia Parson, may the light always shine on you, and may you live long. We thank you for all of the love and support you provide to our marriage. To Dasmond, Dajon (RIP), Douglas III, Drezyn, and Dealo, may we continue to illustrate and model to you all what God can do in your life when you align yourself accordingly. To our grandchildren – Dreshawn, London, and Denim – we love you all and cannot wait to see you fulfill your dreams. To our nieces and nephews, it is incredible watching each of you grow and learn new things. To my siblings, thank you for loving Doug and me. Your support for all my endeavors has been the daily dose I need to push through during life's challenging times.

The love you give to Doug and me is priceless! Thank you to our immediate family, extended family, and friends. We always feel your support and give thanks to our tribe. Last, I want to thank my amazing, funny, loving, adventurous husband. You are my rock, soulmate, cool breeze on a hot day, main man, best friend, and warrior. My love for you is endless! Let's ride this wave, Babe!

Acknowledgements

Thank you….

- To God first for leading and guiding us

- To Clarence KD McNair for his vision and for seeing opportunities for us that we didn't know existed

- To Dr. Ebony Lee (my sister-in-law) for always listening to my cries, screams, and laughter

- To Candee Whitfield for your guidance and authenticity; we are forever grateful.

- Special love to my fierce siblings: Yuri, Dosomu, Tariq, Summaya, and Alia

When I think of Doug and Atiya, the words indestructible *and* perpetual *come to mind. They are indestructible because the strength of their love, partnership, and faith has enabled them to surmount the challenges that have come along their journey as a couple. Additionally, they have a perpetual pursuit to continue growing as a couple so that their marriage and success are not merely status quo. They are striving together to leave an extraordinary legacy. Finally, they are a very giving couple – giving of their time, wisdom, and resources. They receive a lot because they give a lot. Overall, Doug and Atiya have the amazing gift of being able to move in sync; no matter the challenge – they move as ONE UNIT, and this has allowed them to accomplish many goals and have a powerful partnership that's not perfect but always progressing.*
Yuri and Dr. Ebony Lee

Doug and Atiya are two of the most authentic and personable people you'll meet—the true definition of a power couple and game changers in whatever game they decide to play!

When I think of Doug and Atiya, I think about how their relationship started, what they've been through, and where they are today.

It is a true relationship that has stood the test of time. They have found a way to make it work. I'm grateful to witness the journey of their marriage. Best wishes to you both. Love you.
Sam and Erica Cotton

They are the epitome of what a romantic business relationship looks like.
Jasiel "Yung Joc" and Kendra Robinson, Esq.

The Parsons are committed to God, their relationship, their family, their businesses, and each other. The wisdom they bring to all of that from being together for 20+ years makes everything work. They are an unstoppable power couple!
Candee Whitfield, LPC, NCC, DCC-Suddenly! Professional Counseling & Consulting

Introduction

"Love recognizes no barriers. It jumps hurdles, leaps fences, penetrates walls to arrive at its destination full of hope."
– Maya Angelou

Every couple that's been married for a significant amount of time is always asked the same question: *What's the secret to a happy marriage?* There's the traditional advice like *"never go to bed angry"* and the classic reminder that *"marriage requires compromise."* But in order to live happily ever after, your marriage must be a happy one, filled with the kind of deep passion and radical acceptance that cultivates a blissful bond between two people. Our goal is to share our story to inspire other couples. Working together isn't always easy, but having the same goals to build together and compromise makes it smoother.

In this book Doug and I, known by many of our friends and clients as Bricks and Blondie, will give you an all-access pass to the keys that helped us *flip our marriage* from good to amazing. We share with you the keys that we used to identify and celebrate each other's strengths and learn from the mistakes that we made. No marriage is perfect. There is always room for improvement, and we give you the real and raw version of our story because we want you to have the tools you need to flip your relationship into something spectacular. So many of us are looking for the best way to fall in love – or fall back in love – with our significant other. We try to find the keys that other successful couples have used to spice up their marriage, but sometimes, we just can't figure out what they are doing so well. In this book, we cut out the middleman and bring those tips straight to you, so you can experience the bliss that we have together. We have found a way to remain connected and fall deeper in love as we grow together, and we want the same thing for you.

You will hear us use an extended metaphor of *flipping a home* to describe how you can develop a thriving marriage. Doug and I are real estate developers, and that motif of flipping houses will be the lens through which we will describe what we did – and continue to do – in our relationship. When you flip a home, you rehab a property to the point that it is more valuable when you are done than when you purchased it. We took that same approach in our marriage because we took something that was not operating at its best, put the work in to enhance it in every way that we could, and brought in the experts and spiritual guidance to design the best blueprint for our relationship, and made it the dream relationship that we both deserve. Our challenge was seeing the finish line when we began our journey and remembering that the work was worth the result at the end.

We challenge you to see the same value for your flipped relationship as you follow these keys that we outline. We give you step-by-step guidelines to do what we did using each part of the home flipping process. You can't build on shaky soil or with a poor foundation, so we teach you how to make sure that your relationship is stable and secure. We also share what we did to put structure in our relationship as its frame, and we are transparent in our process of putting on a spiritual covering as the roof of our relationship to deter outside influences. We share what we did to include systems of connection in our relationship to ensure that our relationship was working at its top performance. Last, we share how we worked together to accomplish a marriage that is worth more to us now than it was before we started this journey.

As real estate developers who specialize in flipping homes, we give you the real and raw version of our story. One thing that I think you will see is that we don't sugarcoat parts of our journey. Sometimes our path presented unnecessary challenges. We made mistakes along the way. We didn't start out with the right blueprint because we were missing the spiritual covering that we have now. When times got hard early in our relationship, we didn't seek out someone to help us read the blueprints and make sure that we were doing things the right way. We thought we knew what we were doing, like most couples who were unmindful and madly in love. We just thought we would figure it out, and that is when we learned some valuable lessons the hard way.

You get an opportunity to meet Atiya and me in this book, and we are so excited about it. We were nervous at first when we decided to write this book to help other people because we were not sure how people would react to hearing our real story. However, we got over that really quickly. We are who we are, and that ain't going to change after you read this book. We got the nicknames Bricks and Blondie for a reason, and many people know us by those names. Atiya got her name from her blonde hair color that she has had forever, and I got the name Bricks...well, let's just say it came from my prior work in the streets of construction. Now my wife is Dr. Parson, and people call me Doug or Douglas, professionally.

No matter how successful we have been professionally and personally, we are still Bricks and Blondie, Doug and Atiya, from Indianapolis, Indiana. At my core, I am as Indianapolis as you can get, but I think you will see that I am honest about my journey. When I messed up in the past, I tell you because I want you to learn what not to do in certain situations. You will know it is me because I am sharing my thoughts with you in a different font than Atiya. I wanted to stand out in my own way! You will hear from both of us in each chapter, so you can see how we viewed our experiences from different perspectives. We may see things differently sometimes, but at the end of the day, we have always wanted the same end goal.

Like any developer, I am sure that you have scoped out the landscape and selected the property or the person you think is best for you. You did your research and checked the comps. You think that you can make a good profit from this property if you put the work in. Just like you do when you are about to make an investment in a property, you have to keep that same energy in your marriage. You knew the potential when you selected your spouse. You see them for their potential, and you feel that you can make something special together. Don't get turned off when you see that there are issues that you are going to have to address when you get started. Trust me. No flip ever goes according to plan 100% of the time. Something always goes wrong.

Sometimes, we find lead-based paint or asbestos in the home, and we have to get rid of it. That happens in relationships, too, and people have to get rid of toxic elements in their relationships. We may find that the wiring in the home is faulty or there are unforeseen problems with the plumbing or HVAC units, and just like we do in marriage, we do what we have to do to fix it. If you want to see the value of your investment in the end, you have to put in the work, and you cannot rush the process. That is what we believe about our relationship, and we are going to teach you what you can do to experience in your relationship what we have today. Was it always easy? Hell no! Atiya almost left me a few times, but I knew what I had and was willing to do what was needed to flip my marriage. By the end of this book, I know you will be willing to do the same thing for your marriage. Let's get to work!

Chapter 1
The Blueprint—The Beginning: The Evolution of Bricks and Blondie

This journey between Bricks and me started almost 30 years ago in a small town in Indiana called Indianapolis. How could two people from such different backgrounds come together and make magic? Our backgrounds were so different, yet so alike. Our fathers were both addicted to the streets and drugs, and that would later be the downfall of both. Fueled with the blood of hustlers and the drive to be the greatest, our pursuit was born—the pursuit to get it by any means necessary. For me, that meant going to college and making something out of my life, and Bricks, born as Doug, turned to the streets. Our meeting wasn't by happenstance; I feel it happened in Divine order.

One cool evening at the skating rink, my life would forever be changed by this meet-and-greet. I was rolling around the skating rink, minding my own business. Doug just happened to see me, and I caught his eye. It must've been the small waist, thick legs, Guess shorts outfit, and the hair blowing in the breeze. Doug would later reveal that initially, his friend wanted to approach me, but he was too timid. Doug told his friend, "I'll give you a couple of minutes, and if you don't say anything to her, then I will." Later that night, Doug came and introduced himself to me. I remembered him watching me every time I rolled past him. The look of pleasure was on his face as I rolled and crossed each foot over the other, gliding smoothly around the curves. I remember thinking he really wasn't my type. Gold tooth. Braids. I figured he probably was a hustler. I don't know why I thought he was a hustler; it must've been my spidey senses. I believe he waited until we were all leaving, and the car he slid into confirmed my intuition. It looked really expensive and had shiny gold rims.

During this era in my life, most of the guys I knew were hustlers, so I could spot one a mile away. Although Doug did have a nice smile and a welcoming tone to his voice, I was tired of dealing with guys in the streets, so without a second thought, I decided to toss his number.

Then, one day while working at the mall, which was one of three jobs that I had at the time, my car wouldn't start. While I was waiting for someone to come and jump-start my car, you wouldn't believe who came rolling down the aisle! Doug! Once again, he was flashy. Driving a two-door white Lexus coupe with gold rims, he pulled up next to me and smiled, revealing a gold tooth in the front of his mouth. "I have you now," he said with a smirk on his face. "Why didn't you call me?" I was hot and tired from working all day and could barely keep my sundress from ruffling up from the wind. As I clenched the side of my floral summer dress, I told him – in my most convincing voice – that I had lost his number. We exchanged a few words, and I wrote his number down on a crumpled piece of paper in the front seat of my older model red Acura.

From that time on, Doug and I built a friendship. We enjoyed eating at local restaurants and going to entertainment events. Our first

CHAPTER 1: THE BLUEPRINT—THE BEGINNING: THE EVOLUTION OF BRICKS AND BLONDIE

date was actually at Red Lobster on the East side of Indianapolis. Doug was still hustling, and I was finishing my third year of undergraduate school. Doug and I really came from two different worlds. He attended a public school system on the East side of Indianapolis and had three sons already by the age of 21. I didn't have any children, attended a private Montessori school from age four until I was 14, and graduated from a public high school. Our high schools were actually rival schools. I joke with him to this day about how I think my school was better than his. Our religious practices were different as well. Doug grew up practicing Christianity, and I was born a Muslim. Our backgrounds were vastly different, yet these dissimilarities would later establish the foundation for our long-standing bond. So how did two people with such vast differences end up still together for over two decades? Well, it certainly wasn't without several bumps and stops on the road along the way.

For Doug, a chain of serious events would occur to help him change the course of his life. As the saying goes, when you are in the streets, you will end up dead or in jail. Fortunately, neither of these would be Doug's personal fate. He must have many angels watching over him because he was able to leave Indianapolis unscathed. I smile when he often refers to me as one of his angels. One evening in 1995, Doug came home in distress. I can remember the day as if it were yesterday. Doug said he was moving to Lexington, Kentucky, where his aunt and uncle lived at the time. He was going to get a fresh start and make amends with the town he had called home since birth. By this time, we were actually living together because someone had broken into my apartment months prior. As a result, Doug felt it was best for me to move in with him, and since I was over there all the time, it was a no-brainer. And this time would be no different; without hesitation, I decided to go with him.

When I look back, I can't believe I left behind my family and all that I knew. I guess some things are just meant to be. I didn't even tell my family I was leaving until I was already gone. Everyone was initially upset and didn't understand. At the time, they really didn't know Doug that well, so I can understand their apprehension and displeasure with me uprooting my life so hastily. A few days later, we packed up a U-Haul and moved to Lexington, Kentucky. By this time in our relationship, it had been a little over a year, and obviously, our friendship had grown into more of a romance. I think this move made our bond even closer because we were spending so much more time with one another. I applied to and was accepted into the University of Kentucky, where I completed my undergraduate degree in education. Now wait a minute…you didn't think this was a fairytale, and we ran off happily ever after, did you? For the first year or so, being in this relationship was not the best! One of the things that most hustlers have in common is multiple women, and for some, that's hard to shake. We faced this challenge and other challenges that many couples face, and we participated in counseling off and on. The idea of being transparent and getting to know our communication styles became very important.

Our relationship has been tested many times over the years. I remember when we first moved to Kentucky, Doug had to find a job. He worked several jobs as a teenager but never as an adult. His first job in Kentucky was as a bus monitor for one of the school systems. He said he remembered seeing the beautiful houses he passed in the neighborhoods and imagined living in one of those homes one day too. Especially on cold days, he could see the smoke coming out of the chimneys and envisioned the same for his home one day. He also worked at a local car auction washing cars, which was laborious and tiresome, but he was willing to do whatever he had to do not return to the street life. I would pack his meals daily, and people would say, "That smells so good; what is it?" It was probably baked chicken and veggies from the previous night. If nothing else, Doug had great lunches, but he didn't like that job.

During these times, he always saw himself doing something different – but legitimate – that would restore his financial status. He was really in a dark place, and I had to remind him that bad times don't last forever. A few years later, Doug decided to open his own cleaning service. I remember going from door to door, business to business, trying to get new customers. We bought a working van and a few shirts with our logo and began the new journey. You see, breaking new ground wasn't new for us. When you have book smarts coupled with a street or hustler's mentality, anything you seek to accomplish is possible. Doug even went to adult school in Kentucky to finish his high school degree. And yes, he earned it at the age of 22! Although not married yet, we were three years deep into our relationship. It felt like us against the world! We were close enough to get his three sons on the weekends, and they spent most holidays and summers with us too.

We both love children; therefore, we decided to expand the family. Doug was ready for another child, and this would be my first. We were doing better financially, and Doug had invested in his first flip. I definitely wanted to be married before we had children, but I wasn't the type to force the topic of marriage. I can remember the night Doug proposed. We were sitting in the living room and had just finished having dinner. He asked if I wanted some wine and handed me a thin glass. He got on one knee as I began to take a sip of the sparkling white wine and said, "Look at your glass." In the thin glass was a diamond ring at the bottom. I was so excited and, of course, said, "Yes!" I can't lie, I was excited and nervous at the same time. Neither Doug nor I had the best example of a healthy marriage. We were definitely embarking into unfamiliar territory, yet since he was now my best friend, it felt right. As always, it was us against the world, and we would create our own blueprint for a healthy and loving marriage. A month or two later, we also found out I was pregnant with our first child. This was also the year I graduated from my undergraduate program, walking across the stage with my baby bump. We tied the knot on July 3, 1999.

After I graduated from the University of Kentucky as an educator, we decided to move to Atlanta. Our four years in Lexington, Kentucky, had served its purpose; we were now ready to leave our comfort zone. Unbeknownst to us, this would be the start of a new life and career path for Doug. We moved to Atlanta in 2000. The agent we chose to show us homes would become like family. We were so impressed with her skills and caring heart. She took us to her home, and it was absolutely amazing. She talked to Doug about getting his license, and the rest is history.

Well…not quite. Before getting his license, Doug owned a clothing store and recording studio in Georgia. He still had the cleaning business in Kentucky, but he lost a big money-making client, which was Best Buy. When he lost that account, he decided to shut the business down. He circled back around and decided to go to real estate school. Doug getting his license was the start of it all. It wasn't easy in the beginning, though. He struggled with making cold calls to potential clients and securing new clients. We were struggling financially and often relied on my income from teaching. That's what love and marriage are all about – helping one another during the ups and downs. Doug and I have always been business-minded, and the word partnership is important. Balancing career and marriage can certainly have its highs and lows.

CHAPTER 1: THE BLUEPRINT—THE BEGINNING: THE EVOLUTION OF BRICKS AND BLONDIE

We decided to have another child, and our second son as a couple was born in 2001. With more responsibility came the need to grow more financially stable as well. There were times when Doug had to pawn things in order to get gas and a haircut. He often reminisces on the times I would just put money in his car for him to find later. For this, he says he will always be grateful. There were lots of times when I had to cover all of the expenses and even had to sell a car or two. Yes, Doug would buy me a car but end up having to sell it. He always bought me something better the next time. For us, it's never been about 50/50. It's about making sure we, as a whole, are climbing and accomplishing goals.

I had been teaching for numerous years, and Doug was starting to make headway in the real estate world. As most people know, real estate has its series of ups and downs. You have your good days and your not-so-good days. You definitely have to be in grind mode. Just when things were starting to get better for us as a whole, something life-changing happened. This was the first event and the start of the transformation I would continue to witness in Doug. In 2013, we experienced a devastating loss that changed our lives forever. We lost Dajon, my stepson, who had the kindest spirit, wittiest personality, and deepest love for his brothers and family. He died as a result of gun violence. It's a day that will be forever engraved in our minds. I can remember that day as if it were yesterday. He had been missing since the previous day, and I went to work the next day feeling uneasy, not knowing what happened to him. Later that day, I received a phone call that he was found deceased. Gun violence in Indianapolis was an issue then and still is to this day. That was also one of the factors that drove us away years prior. Looking back, I don't know how Doug made it. Losing a child is devastating, and this was a pivotal moment for Doug. Gradually, I began to see a softer side of him, a new zest for life, and a need to explore more. He had already changed many of his ways from the street days, but there was beginning to be an even softer side of him emerging.

We often talk about life and the decisions that people make. For me, I saw a man go from being good to great before my eyes. Prior to Dajon's passing, Doug and I experienced a rough patch in our relationship. I really didn't know if we would make it over this hurdle. Sometimes, it's better to be still, pray, and let God lead you in the right direction. For some reason, saving our relationship felt bigger than me. It's hard to explain. My heart was broken; his trust and loyalty were in question. Yet, I still felt like Doug needed me. Then, when Dajon passed, I understood the bigger picture. No one else would have the history with him that I did. No one else would've been able to comfort him during this time. Fast forward to July 2018, and our family was hit with another devastating tragedy. There's a saying that my elders would always proclaim: "God isn't going to put anything on your plate that you can't handle." Well, just when I thought our plate would not overflow, nine family members died tragically in the Missouri Duck Boat incident. After learning of the tragedy, we paced back and forth all afternoon, awaiting further developments from the news. Soon after, we would learn the devastating fates of our loved ones. Doug's cousins, aunt, and uncles had all died. This was when I surely knew he would break. His faith had been tested by the deaths of his father and his son, and now this.

But once again, he would stand the test of time, and eventually, I began to see an even softer side. He drew closer to me and developed more spiritually. He now had several more angels watching and protecting him. He dug deeper into his craft, and our time together became more intentional and purposeful.

CHAPTER 1: THE BLUEPRINT—THE BEGINNING: THE EVOLUTION OF BRICKS AND BLONDIE

Fast forward to the last 10 years. Doug sold his first house to a local celebrity in Atlanta. This was after years of selling and grinding. From there, it was on because he started to get referrals for other celebrities. Now, in addition to being called "Bricks," he is known as the "Celebrity Realtor." I was slowly moving from assistant to partner. I listened for years to Doug talking to different clients on the phone and thought the business was interesting, but I didn't have the desire to become licensed. I preferred working behind the scenes. I made sure the paperwork was done for the flips. Doug had been persistent for many years, finally convincing me to get licensed. Trust me; it was not easy, but with most things in life that are great, it takes work. I needed my license so that we could build this empire and legacy. Remember, I was slowly coming from behind his shadow into my own. Doug went from flipping bricks in the streets of Indianapolis to flipping "bricks" with houses. There are many late nights when we stay up strategizing and creating master plans. You see, to become a household name, your household needs to be in order. We stay prayed up, receive counseling when needed, communicate openly, and remain transparent with one another. Where we are going, we don't need any fumbles or mishaps.

We recognize that each of us brings individual talents, strengths, and weaknesses. How will we complement and uplift one another? Doug has an *I don't care what people think about me* type of attitude, which can be an asset in the real estate business because the market can be so competitive. However, I am very cautious about what people think or may say about me. I am meticulous and conscious about my words and observe before speaking. There's definitely a time and place for both in real estate. Being business partners and married requires deliberate actions. A partnership is somewhat like a marriage because each person has specific roles. We have too much on our plate, and it's an unproductive use of time to not speak to one another! There's no way you can be angry with one another…stay mad and get ready for a power move. It's just not that simple! Doug has learned to respect our boundaries, be transparent, and know who's in charge…me!

I figured that she would say that, but Atiya knows who's really in charge, behind the scenes. She isn't going to tell you the whole story like it happened. She was my assistant for like 20 years, and she has been trying to run the business this whole time. Even when she was at work with her students in the classroom, she always gave me her ideas for the business on the sly. For probably 10 years, I begged her to get her real estate license and leave the classroom, but she refused. I knew she had a passion for real estate and fixing and flipping houses, so I just figured I might as well get her to come on board since she feels she is my boss anyway. In all seriousness, I learned that Atiya brings a lot to the table in our business to help us grow that I wouldn't have thought of. I am always focused on grinding, meeting new clients, starting new projects, and growing the business. However, when I convinced her to take that two-week course and get her real estate license, she brought her educational background to what we do. She has this way of relating to our clients like a teacher, adding another level to what we offer our clients. Let me give you an example.

Atiya knew that one of my passions was flipping houses. I was good at it, and I knew it. However, people kept coming up to me and asking me if I could teach them to flip houses, and I didn't have the time or patience to do that. She'd just gotten her license and wanted to find a way to jump in with me and help me, so she decided to get involved with mentoring our clients. Let me tell you this. She found her passion in mentoring our new flipping clients. She and I worked together to take them under our wings, and through her teaching

CHAPTER 1: THE BLUEPRINT—THE BEGINNING: THE EVOLUTION OF BRICKS AND BLONDIE

power, we have become skilled at making the flipping process plain for them and guiding them to get really good at this flipping game.

I really was not as excited as you would think to start a new venture and take a real estate course when I finally listened to Doug, because I felt that I was all tested out. I already went through that harrowing process of obtaining my Ph.D., and there was no way I wanted to get back into school – it didn't matter if it was real estate school – and take another high-stakes test like I did to finish my dissertation. However, Doug can be convincing when he wants to be, and I figured that I might want to try my hand at something new and see how well we could do if we worked together officially.

What Doug didn't mention is that when I started working with him in full-fledged real estate, I was only three years from retirement. I began to see the finish line in one career and the starting point for another passion of mine. I had to figure out where to jump into the business and help him grow it. After some reflection, I found that I could be most impactful in the area of mentoring. Something is rewarding about making things plain for people who are struggling to understand. It reminded me of why I love teaching. I saw the clients as my students and put the same effort into teaching them about mentorship that I did with the students I love. Most people need guidance when they begin flipping houses because they are not ready to do it independently. They may have read about it or seen shows on television that teach house-flipping principles, but based on our experience, they still needed to learn the fundamentals with expert guidance.

We teach them the whole process of searching for homes, buying the homes, doing walkthroughs of a home, running comps to determine if the flip will be profitable, setting a sale price, and closing.

We love it! We have connected to the teaching and mentorship process so well that we are strongly considering expanding our reach into the education sector by developing a career pathway for real estate. Through these course offerings, high school students can learn about this industry early on. This may be particularly insightful for those young people who either don't want to go to college or may still be uncertain about their post-secondary endeavors, yet they are looking for a way to make money. With early exposure to this industry, students may find their passion in real estate.

My doctorate is in Curriculum and Instruction, and we feel that there should be a program that enables students to obtain industry credentials in real estate during their high school years. This is often the case in other career pathways (e.g., healthcare science, cosmetology, auto mechanics). We know that we have the passion and the knowledge to teach adults and young people about the real estate game, and we plan on grooming the next level of real estate entrepreneurs to become successful investors, developers, and agents. Flipping houses is what's hot, and we have the game on lock —thus the title of Doug's best-selling book, *The Art of Flipping Bricks*.

I wish they had real estate classes like Atiya is describing during my time in high school. Most people don't recognize how much their lives would change if they could learn these skills we teach before they graduate from high school. Nowadays, so many of these young people have their own goals and agendas, and a program like what we are going to develop for them would go great with their goals. I wish I had people who looked like me to tell me about the possibilities in real estate when I was in high school. I bought my first house when I was 19 in Indianapolis. However, I didn't really understand the importance of homeownership or having real estate. I just had the means to buy it and needed a place to call home. Since I was in the streets then, my parents weren't for me bucking the house rules. Things I didn't learn in school, we now try and instill in people. We teach people in layman's terms what they need to know, which makes our work together so impactful. An added bonus is we are also building a legacy, and now our sons are interested in real estate.

Once Doug and I found a way to work together to incorporate what I still love to do in the classroom with his passion for real estate and house flipping, our journey as partners began.

KEYS TO HELP YOU FLIP YOUR MARRIAGE

- There is a person whom God uniquely designed just for you.

- Your friendship with your partner should undergird your relationship.

- Your experiences in your relationship develop the depth and strength that will sustain it.

- Each partner brings strengths, talents, and areas for improvement into the relationship.

- Find out what your partner does that inspires you, and encourage that behavior.

- Flipping a marriage into what it can become potentially requires hard work and effort.

Chapter 2
Time to Build: Break Ground with Us!

Your marriage should last a lifetime, but it depends on how it's built and who you marry. I don't think that any couple dates for a prolonged period of time, designs an elaborate wedding ceremony, takes vows before God and family members, and plans to get divorced long after they get married. That would be a massive waste of time and resources. Couples plan to get married because they want to spend a lifetime together, so it is essential to think long-term when considering your relationship and do whatever it takes. Just like the story of the "Three Little Pigs," your marriage needs to be strong enough to withstand the attacks that the enemy will throw at it to test you and your partner.

The strength of your marriage also depends on the type of soil that exists where you choose to build your home. You must choose the right setting just like you choose the right person because if you make an error in that crucial part of your life, the consequences could be devastating. What materials you use matter. Details matter. No house or marriage is going to be perfect, either. As I shared earlier, our journey was anything but typical, and we come from very different backgrounds. However, what we have in common are the materials that make us great together. We know our roles and respect each other for what we bring to the table. I respected the hard work I witnessed Doug investing in his business and worked diligently to support him in whatever way I could.

If you know Doug, you know that he has his way of interacting with his clients. I noticed that he could be a little rough with them. As a hustler, you learn to have tough skin in some situations in order to survive. He can be an acquired taste for some people. It is like you have to take him straight, no chaser. He tells them things exactly as they are, and I am convinced that he doesn't think twice about how they receive what he is saying. The people who have become accustomed to how he communicates don't pay it much attention because they know that he knows what he is talking about. They recognize that at the end of the rehab or renovation process, Doug is going to transform their space into something beautiful. I use that same approach in our marriage because I know his heart, so when he doesn't sugarcoat things like me to make them easier to process, I allow my brain to transcribe what he said into much more flowery language, and I move on. I can say that he has gotten better with his delivery over the years. He is more conscious of what and how he says it before verbalizing it. I am the complete opposite of him, but when we are together, our energies just match, and we work well together. We know how to play off each other, and I think our clients recognize our individual strengths in our business and our mutual respect for each other in terms of how we interact with each other and with them.

When you build or renovate a house, there are steps that you have to take first. Preparation is key, and it is the same thing with a marriage. If I could go back and do things over again, before we got

CHAPTER 2: TIME TO BUILD: BREAK GROUND WITH US!

married I would have taken more time with premarital counseling. We learned so many things from trial and error that I wish we knew before we got married. We would have laid down a better blueprint for our relationship, and I think that would have prevented or minimized a lot of the challenges that we experienced needlessly. That is water under the bridge now, but those premarital steps of really learning one another and figuring out how to work through the problems that naturally occur would have been ideal. Similarly, in a home flipping project, there are many things that happen behind the scenes that we discuss before venturing into a project, or should I say breaking ground. You do not start demoing a home when you first enter the front door. It is not like it looks on a television show where they purchase, demo, and renovate a home in a 60-minute television program. You must plan your renovation project in advance, decide what parts need to be removed or renovated, and outline a plan to rebuild the home into a better state. In relationships, it's natural to have barriers when your feelings have been compromised. Together, you need to decide what needs to be repaired or removed to give your relationship the best chance to survive and thrive. In order to forgive, heal, and move on, those walls must come down. It is a very similar process to renovating a home, and the results can be amazing.

When we renovate a home, Doug and I have different roles in the process. I do like working on my own sometimes, because Doug likes to check on what I'm doing and sometimes gets in my way. He just can't help it, but I know it comes from a place of love. My specialty in the flips mostly consists of doorknobs and electrical plates. People don't realize that the finishing touches on a home can make all the difference because they show potential buyers that you care about the details. That is my area, but sometimes, Doug just won't let me be great, and he finds a way to try and control that aspect of the flip too. The one time I had him pick up my items was the last time he did so. He did not get the right knobs; however, he wants to tell me how to do my tasks. Hilarious! I just have to sit back and laugh.

Building our roles came from recognizing what each of us brings into the relationship. I think that we incorporate aspects from each other's skill sets, and that has made us even more effective as an entrepreneurial power couple. Doug likes to sit back and just watch what he's created. He thinks I am a mini version of him when it comes to flipping. I think he believes I am one of his greatest creations when he watches me work – essentially, his masterpiece. I'd like to see some of my polish rub off on him so that he becomes a better communicator with our clients, because he has watched how I interact with them. When he gives me a suggestion for ways to flip a property, I listen to his vision for the property. Of course, we know it takes some convincing at first, but when I get into it, I am all in. Breaking ground for me on a project symbolizes breaking down walls, and I get excited about the home's potential. I feel that same excitement when I see that he and I have breakthroughs in our relationship because I recognize our potential together, even in the midst of challenging periods of our marriage.

I have watched Atiya with some of our clients. She is so gentle and kind to them, and when I really sat back and listened to her, I realized that they respond very well to her. I couldn't believe how effective she was with them when she used her soft and kind tone to guide and mentor them. I started to think that I might want to adopt some of her approaches in what I am doing because I might get even more sales and even find repeat customers who enjoyed their experience so much with me that they want to buy another home or refer me to someone else. Because I accepted what Atiya brings to the table, and we incorporated her approach into what we do, our business continued to flourish. I have several repeat customers now and even referrals from those same people. I have found that even my celebrity clients don't have the structure or understanding they need to buy a home, and when they follow the guidance that we provide, they are able to be successful and buy the homes of their dreams.

No one had to tell me that I was a little rough around the edges. Everyone could not take my blunt honesty about what I thought should happen with a flip, but that is because I know what the hell I am doing. I think that people kind of liked my honesty because they never had to ask where I stood on what I was telling them. I just gave it to them raw, but Atiya used to always tell me that I needed to have more finesse in my approach. I had no idea what she was talking about because I was still making money. I didn't really care if someone didn't choose to go through with a project with me because my business was booming. However, I did notice that after I convinced her to come on board and help me with my clients, things got a lot easier for me. Previously, I was fine with being myself because I made money wherever I was in my life, but with her, I was making even more money. They say that you can catch more flies with honey than with vinegar, and Atiya is the best example of that I have ever seen. She just has this way about her that gets her in doors with clients that I might not have been able to open.

Once I saw what she brought to the table, I realized it was time to work! We started planning how we were going to revamp the business to ensure that we expanded our appeal. We began to work as a team, and she told me how she wanted to work with me in her area of expertise to help me secure more clients and bigger projects. Atiya and I had to decide how we were going to make sure that we were effective when we were working together and expanding our footprint in the business. Being effective would allow us to avoid projects that would become more of a headache than a profitable venture, similar to avoiding building on soil that is unstable.

It is not as easy as you think when you decide to go into business with your spouse. I had to be much more intentional with my planning for projects when we started flipping together. Before she came on board, it was just me, and I did whatever I wanted from the start of a project to the finish. I didn't have any other general contractors on the project. Now she wanted to help me with the finishing touches to the projects, and as much as I wasn't sure how I was going to like giving her that control over the homes, I knew that she knew what the hell she was doing. I also had to make sure that we found ways to leave work at work when it was time to clock out every day.

I had a horrible work-life balance, which was an issue from the beginning of our relationship. She liked the fact that I worked hard and took care of my family, but I had all kinds of problems turning it off. Atiya wanted the foundation of our business to be the strength of our marriage, and it's a good thing we were and continue to be connected outside of our work together. Before we were business partners, we were friends, lovers, and soul mates, and that's how we have been able to sustain our relationship together for so long.

When I am considering purchasing a home, one of the things my team does for me is check all the major parts of the home. Some homes have significant issues that make the purchase not worth it. A couple of major issues are, sometimes the floors not being leveled, or major leaks. Water leaks erode the drywall in the home, causing black mold. If those problems are not addressed, they can damage or destroy a home over time. Not having the right safeguards to protect your marriage from issues constantly eroding your relationship's foundation can be devastating.

Your home would not last long if the gutters didn't drain water away from its foundation, and if the ground wasn't pitched properly, water would pool around your home and destroy the foundation over time. We recognized early in our marriage that stability in our relationship was important. I couldn't expect that anything else about our relationship would go well if I built our marriage on unstable ground. The soil that was under our foundation had to be right, so we could start building our life together.

I had to learn to maintain my marriage by paying attention to Atiya's needs and protecting our good soil from being washed away by storms. She loved it when I showed her that I loved her in different ways, like giving her flowers and paying attention to her needs. I learned that I needed to prioritize her, and everything would be amazing between us. I married up for sure when we got together, so I had to invest in maintaining my marriage just like I maintained and restored properties. Our foundation had to be my top priority, and when we began working together, I learned more reasons why she was created uniquely for me. I had to let her be her, and I needed to continue strengthening our foundation, so we could grow together. We invested in our relationship by removing walls that existed in our communication, laying a spiritual blueprint to strengthen our union, and building our marriage on soil that was fertile.

I also learned that you can't use cheap finishes when your project is done. You must plan out every part of the project before you break ground, and that includes envisioning the end product for your project. Atiya brought a different element to our relationship because she sees the details that I don't see. She knows what will "pop" for the customers to take them over the hump and get them to buy the home. I am very detail-oriented too, and know, for instance, which light fixtures will be great in the home. We enjoy going on our supply runs at the local stores. It's a comedy show for sure every time, and Atiya likes to record me taking my sweet time. It's all about the small details you put in a house. That also exists in the small details of our relationship. Atiya is a great judge of character when it comes to people, and I had to learn that if she doesn't like someone for any reason, it is probably because she sees something in them that I don't see. I didn't trust her "spidey sense" at first when she would tell me that she didn't feel a person in her spirit. However, I learned that she sees the details about people, and she senses their spirit.

I learned that if she thinks they are putting on a facade for us personally or professionally, I should trust her judgment. That is why you pick well when you marry your partner because they play to your strengths. I am a big-picture guy. My role is important because I know what I want a project to be, just like I know how I want my marriage to look. But in addition to the big picture, I get into all the minor details because I am focused on potential. I know what I need to do to break ground on a project and flip it the right way. However, I need someone like Atiya to slow my process down and make sure that I don't miss the details sometimes. It wasn't always easy for me to shift my thinking and see my need for her approach, but I am glad that I have changed my thinking. In our work together and in our marriage, I benefit from her helping me to establish a blueprint including the small but important things. I also have become a better husband and entrepreneur because she helps me figure out what barriers I need to remove and walls I need to build on the front end to help me improve what I already do well.

Marriage is supposed to be forever, which is why you choose the person who best complements your weaknesses and helps you to be your best. You must be intentional about the soil on which you choose to build your relationship. Doug and I had to learn what each other's strengths were, and we learned how to become great together. We focused on building our marriage on good soil and asked God to undergird our relationship. We also learned how to focus on the details of our marriage, which helped us to tear down things that divided us and build barriers whenever necessary to protect our connection. We realized how we could protect the soil around our foundation by diverting away any distractions or people who wanted to erode the soil under our marriage. This intentional effort took work, but in the end, our marriage is amazingly stronger because of it. I appreciated my husband for identifying my professional strengths that could help him grow his business. I know it brought us closer together because I felt valued and wanted. I help him finish the projects and close deals, and we have become a power couple together because we are intentional about working together as a unit.

KEYS TO HELP YOU FLIP YOUR MARRIAGE

- Marriage is designed to be amazing with your forever partner.

- The right soil is essential to build a strong foundation for your marriage.

- Prevent people and things from washing away the soil under your relationship.

- Choose the right person who encourages you to grow and develop.

- Have fun together and find opportunities to laugh *with* your spouse.

- Focus on the details of your connection that will help each of you thrive.

Chapter 3
A Strong Foundation: You Can't Build Without One

A good marriage, like a well-built house, needs a strong foundation. Stabilize the house and the relationship. Rather than lasting a lifetime as a treasure, a house would be untenable if built on a faulty foundation. So, too, is the fate of a marriage built on a faulty foundation. A home that has a proper foundation serves dual purposes. It protects what you can see above the ground and prevents damage from moisture, cold, and earth-shifting below the home. Similarly, in marriage, having a strong foundation between a husband and wife, especially a couple who is in business together, is important because it ensures that what you see on the outside matches the strength that exists in the areas of their relationship that you can't see.

As Doug's career continued to grow and progress as a home flipper, real estate agent, and developer, many people only knew the side of him that they saw. He is very personable and fun, and his energy attracts people to him. Many of his clients did not know the role that I played as his foundation to ensure that he was able to be successful in what he did. As a mom, I helped raise our two children, and I was his default assistant for most of the time that he was building his company in Atlanta. He and I would discuss all aspects of his business, and he included me in his decisions because he trusted my opinion and my growing skills with real estate.

Doug saw me as an asset to what he wanted his company to become, which is why he pushed me toward getting my real estate license. It's funny; I can remember his late father, Douglas Sr., telling him not to mess up his relationship with me. An asset, indeed, is probably what his father would've said. I know Doug misses his long conversations with him, but his father has his own special way of still communicating.

Doug felt that we could be a power couple together, and he valued my skills as an educator to give his business something that it didn't have. He trusted me, and because we had grown so much as a couple through the difficult times and the times that we didn't have much early on in our journey, he knew that we could accomplish anything together. In all honesty, the development of our spiritual foundation ebbed and flowed, and it was not a smooth journey. Doug had to learn his role as the leader and protector of our family, and I had to learn how to support him while holding him accountable. I knew my husband came from the streets of Indianapolis when I met him. He was hustling back then, and one of the things that has made him as successful as he has been in real estate is his ability to network and connect with others. They call him "Doug the Plug" for a reason. He is connected to everyone, and he has never met a stranger. Everywhere we go, people know him, and they want to be connected to him.

Doug has a natural energy that is irresistible to people, but sometimes, he doesn't see that everyone who wants to come into our

CHAPTER 3: A STRONG FOUNDATION: YOU CAN'T BUILD WITHOUT ONE

circle is not there with good intentions. He loves the limelight and the action that real estate provides. He wants to be with the people and in the mix of all that is going on, but in that same energy, he sometimes misses the fact that there are people there who want my role in his life. They see him as a person with whom they want to connect, and he has had to learn over time that he is the foundation of our home, which means that he has to be strong, make good decisions, and evaluate what situations are not profitable for what we are trying to build personally and professionally. Doug has made huge strides in this area in our marriage, and I think that is why we have been able to grow. We've grown more professionally and spiritually, and are closer as a couple.

As our marriage continued to evolve and develop, I knew that I needed Atiya to be with me in the next phase of my journey. I had many goals for my business, and I needed her eye and her wisdom to give my business another edge. Plus, women have this way of seeing things that men don't see, and I knew that she would make sure that she protected what we had built from negative influences and people who didn't have our best interests in mind. Now, I don't want to suggest that going into business together full-time is always easy, but when you have a wife who is a stabilizing influence and who knows the ins and outs of your business, it definitely makes things much easier. She showed me over many years that she was willing to do whatever it took to grow our company, so it made sense for me to ask her to come on board full-time. She's always been my angel. It's like whatever she touches turns to gold, and her presence protects me. I have so many angels now, especially after losing nine family members at one time. This was a time in my life that I will never forget. Having them as angels has fueled me to have a greater appreciation for life and the time I have with my wife and family.

Our spiritual connection is something that has helped our marriage to grow and develop as our company expands. We were raised in two different faiths, but our commitment to each other, treating others kindly and with respect, and being spiritually connected has helped the foundation of our relationship become stronger. There is no way I could have done what I am doing without her. She is the unsung hero of what we are building together, but I had to trust her and know she brings something to our business that I don't have. This isn't any different from the partnership between a husband and a wife. It is added value when one spouse is strong in an area in which the other person is weak.

With fame and success in my business came a whole host of other challenges. Many people have no idea how challenging it can be to run a successful multi-million-dollar real estate business when you have people around you, especially females who are drawn to your energy and are trying to get close to you. Some of these women are drawn to successful men and the energy that they put out, and I had to learn really early that I had to remain focused on what I was doing professionally. It was a mindset shift for me for real because I come from a hustling mindset, and I am drawn naturally to all that comes along with that lifestyle.

Atiya represents for me the other side of life and the way things should be when I keep first things first and remain dedicated to and focused on my business. I have talked about the importance of developing boundaries a lot in my life, and that was not something that I did very well. I just let people have access to me because I felt that I was helping them, and I must admit that I enjoyed the attention. However, when you are trying to build something great and you want to take your life and your business to the next level, you know that your foundation is very important in that process.

CHAPTER 3: A STRONG FOUNDATION: YOU CAN'T BUILD WITHOUT ONE

Nowadays, I imagine how my actions will make my wife feel, and I know that I have to make different choices. We learned about boundaries from going to counseling. I would personally suggest all married couples seek someone to talk to, and I stand on that!

Over time, I learned the importance of my role as the foundation of our marriage, and I had to become a Godly man and protect her heart from any hurt, danger, or pain. This meant that I had to be extra careful with the people with whom I associated and the situations in which I placed myself. In fact, I think the growth that both of us experienced as we merged our lives and business together was overwhelmingly centered on my individual improvement. She relied on me to anchor our lives, and I had to learn the importance of being the spiritual foundation in our home, not just the breadwinner. I know that I am not in the streets anymore, running around and meeting all different types of women. I understand the importance of having her as my foundation to both my life and my business, and I am certain that this shift in my thinking is what has helped my business to grow. My wife anchored me and stabilized me on my way to the top, and I understand more and more as I experience success the critical role she played in my life and my growth.

I want to illustrate why a strong marriage needs a good foundation. Just like you would not build your dream home on a shaky and uneven foundation, you can't grow your marriage on a foundation that is not strong. When you think of the reasons that a home needs a strong foundation, here are a few things to remember. Your foundation supports your home, resists movement from the ground, insulates your home to maintain an even temperature, keeps moisture out of the home, and prevents insects from getting inside your home. These five functions are important, and they are equally important in marriage. Your foundation supports your home, especially when it experiences earthquakes, strong winds and storms, and bears the overall weight of the structure. In our almost 30 years of being together, there were plenty of storms that we weathered – financial setbacks, disagreements, trust issues, and more. Through all of that, we still chose one another and our marriage. We also committed to building a marriage that was a good example for our children.

A strong foundation resists movement from the ground, especially when challenges come. I have had my faith in our marriage tested. I mentioned earlier that our life together was not always ideal. We experienced some challenges that I didn't think we would be able to survive. He realized that I was committed to him and his growth, and I believe that my support for him forced him to change and grow because he understood how my role helped him to become our foundation.

Family is very important to us. We often talk about children needing a village for support – well, so do adults. It's important for us to have a strong support system, and many of our friends and family look up to us. As we rely on others for support and guidance, you do so when setting your foundation to build. The blueprint for building a home requires a skilled architect. Additionally, when you are flipping a house, it takes skills and vision, imagining the finished product and having the right team. Sometimes building a solid marriage takes a skilled therapist to assist you with the strength of your marriage. There's nothing wrong with going to counseling. As a matter of fact, Doug was very hands-on when choosing our current counselor. I gave him the opportunity to pick the person he wanted, so there wouldn't be any excuse not to go.

CHAPTER 3: A STRONG FOUNDATION: YOU CAN'T BUILD WITHOUT ONE

We still use her from time to time as maintenance. Just like you have upkeep on a house, it works the same in your marriage.

I want to speak on this one because a strong foundation definitely helps us maintain an even keel with each other. Yes, she is right about counseling too. I think I gave her the shock of her life when I agreed to go to counseling. I was willing to do whatever it took to make my marriage better, even if it meant that I had to go out of my comfort zone. I knew that she was worth it, so I dove headfirst into the process and committed myself to becoming the man she needed me to be.

I don't care what anyone says, marriage is not always easy, but it is worth it. I feel like a lot of people give up on their marriage too fast. If someone in the marriage makes one mistake, then it's over! If you can work through your mistakes, at the end, it can be so beautiful. For my wife and me, counseling brought us closer. I haven't been perfect, and when writing this book, I wasn't sure how much she would feel comfortable sharing. I own my mistakes, and I'm so grateful my angel didn't give up on me. My wife and I have different personalities, but where one of us is weak, the other person is strong. I am very playful, and I joke a lot, but she is able to buckle down and make sure that business gets handled while she enjoys herself. She watches our back and front, and I understand her role in ensuring that we always remain who we are supposed to be. She respects me for my personality and how others experience me and want to partner with me, and I respect the fact that she is organized and always very professional. I know that our business benefits from what she brings to it.

Atiya is important to me in our marriage and business because she also helps keep moisture and insects out of our marriage. Let me say that I have learned to be a better man because of her. I was so used to moving and shaking in these streets, and I wasn't watching my back all the time. I am sure she felt like anyone could access me because I was so friendly to everyone, and that approach could have cost me in the long run. When she began to notice and tell me that some of the things that I was doing were impacting her negatively, I had to make a choice about whether I wanted to be the husband, protector, and provider that she needed me to be. I knew that I needed her professionally to help me grow my business, but I also needed her even more to help me to assume the role that I was designed to play emotionally. I am so thankful that we have found our marital synergy, and I am able to move as I was designed to move as the leader of our home. Let me break that down for all the guys out there wondering what "synergy" means. This means my wife and I can accomplish more together than apart. For me, I absolutely wouldn't be where I am today without her. Remember, it doesn't matter how good your home or your marriage looks on the outside to other people, if your foundation is not built to withstand storms, prevent outside influences, and last against the storms that will come in life, your home and your marriage will not survive.

KEYS TO HELP YOU FLIP YOUR MARRIAGE

- The right foundation will cause the relationship to thrive and grow because it is Divinely protected.

- Building a strong foundation means that you make good decisions and protect your partner.

- Identify and build upon the things that your partner does to strengthen you.

- Eliminate any distractions that interfere with the strong foundation in your marriage that you are building.

- Seek God's guidance and wise counsel as you develop and grow your marriage.

- Your relationship will be tested, but if you invest in a strong foundation, it will withstand tests and trials.

Chapter 4
Framing Your House and Marriage to Stand the Test of Time

The framing is the communication between the both of you. If the communication isn't there, then there is no framing. Every relationship needs communication; this is what builds the shape and support of the relationship. Guess what…ish happens. No relationship is shatterproof, like a window. When a contractor puts the frame together, it takes two people. Those two people work together, and each person takes turns holding the pieces that are hammered together. In our relationship, we work together, assisting one another with our day-to-day tasks and business. The nails for the frame are important. The nails stabilize or secure the wood pieces together. Just like the nails secure the frame, a relationship is held together by several factors – time, transparency, and communication, to name a few. You can build a home without the frame, but the home or the relationship probably will not stand without those components.

Doug and I experienced the importance of having a strong framework in our relationship, and let me tell you something: Once we figured out how his strengths and my strengths could support the vision that we shared, we realized that nothing could stop us or stand in our way.

We both have strong ties to family. Doug is an only child, and I have five other siblings. As you can imagine, our perspectives on family and communication can differ at times. I am used to playing in the sandbox with five other people, but his childhood experience was totally different. I would say that before things became much better in our relationship and our communication, I think that Doug was rather selfish. He was primarily concerned with what made him happy, and my happiness and what I needed from him came second. At least, that was my perception; sometimes our perception becomes our reality. I think it was hard for him to understand what marrying someone meant. Living with a spouse and caring for her needs means being intentional. He was so used to being alone and worried about himself first. I believe that this was an area in which I was able to help him learn and grow the most. He didn't have the communication skills, at first, to prioritize me as his wife. He was missing the importance of the nails in our home, and that was something that he worked hard to learn. I didn't think that he was going to take my request seriously for us to go to counseling so that we could become better communicators with each other. As you would expect, I was worried about the strength of the framework of our marriage because we were speaking two different languages, and I didn't think he would ever understand how his actions affected me. I picked up my entire life and moved from my hometown to be with him and support him, and he was struggling to do the most basic thing that I thought he should be able to do easily – communicate with me in a way that made me feel wanted and valued.

If you have ever watched a television program that shows them putting up the skeleton of the home, you know that that process is called completing the *rough framing*. That is when they put together the floor system, the walls, and the roof. That is one of the most critical parts of the home-building process because if the walls are not level or joined together with the right supports (the nails), the home could collapse at any moment. There is a team of people who work together to hold the beams and the frame in place as they are fastened together. No one person can do that job alone. When the construction team has disagreements or is not on the same page, they return to the blueprints to refocus and take a different approach to fix the issue. They have the same goal of building the home, but sometimes, they face obstacles that require them to change their plan.

In our marriage, we used counseling to help us identify potential pitfalls and challenges, but it was still up to us to work together when we left the office and address what we identified as problematic. If we wanted our marriage to grow and our business relationship to improve, we had to be willing to do the work, and I was surprised and encouraged at how dedicated Doug was to the entire process.

When a construction team is building a home, the contractor, framers, and carpenters must work together to complete this process, which is the same expectation for an effective marriage. Doug and I learned which nails (communication strategies) worked best for us, and we learned to listen to each other and find ways to include each other in everything we did. Just like contractors can't skimp on the process and use the cheapest materials to build a high-quality home, we had to invest in our growth, and the results exceeded our expectations astronomically. I gained an even greater respect for Doug as a leader and a businessman the more I worked with him, and I think he saw how much I could help him grow as a husband and expand his company as a real estate agent and developer. The more we communicated with each other, the more we realized that we could do so much more together than we could do apart, and that was the time in our marriage when we realized just how powerful we were as a couple.

As a man and the protector of my home, I had to learn how to communicate better with my wife. When you grow up in the streets, and you are used to a much faster-paced lifestyle, it is not always as easy to think with a team-first mindset. Sometimes, I know I reverted back to my old way of thinking, and I did what was best for me without considering how my actions impacted my wife. I had this beautiful woman who was ten-toes down for me, and I was more worried about myself and my image with the people who knew me sometimes. I was not as sensitive or in tune with her needs as I should have been. I am so thankful that she stuck with me through the thick and thin times and showed her commitment to our marriage. I don't care who you are. You are going to face some difficult times in your marriage. There is a reason that they make shatterproof windows in modern homes. Designers know that things will be launched against them, and they need to withstand just about anything, whether those things are financial troubles, outside influences, pride, disagreements, etc. In those moments when our marriage was tested, I learned just how committed she was to me and how strong we were when we worked together. The more we worked together to become a real estate power couple, the more successful we were in this business. I started to value her for her skill set and how she related to our clients, and she learned more about the business from watching me. We started pulling together even more in the same direction, and it didn't take much time for me to see that nothing could stop us from reaching our dreams.

CHAPTER 4: FRAMING YOUR HOUSE AND MARRIAGE TO STAND THE TEST OF TIME

I definitely say that our love for each other is the nails holding our marriage and business together. Each day, we wake up and go to work, thinking about how we can support each other emotionally and professionally. My wife and I go to each other about everything, and this approach has been much more effective. I used to think she didn't understand what I did for a living, but when she took my encouragement and invested in her real estate class, I saw she could thrive in this business. She showed me that she was willing to support me and my dreams, and I started to value her opinions and her advice about growing my business – and now our business – even more.

One thing I love about my wife is that she lets me be me. That is not the easiest thing to do in marriage, much less in business, but she understood that I do best when I am comfortable and able to work with people in my own way. I knew that her suggestions would only help me improve as a man and as a professional, and we learned to respect and value each other in many different ways.

We learned that the frame of our home and the materials that are used to bring it together are essential in a great marriage. The purpose of the structural framing of the home is to ensure that the home is strong enough to bear the weight of the walls and roof and make sure that the home is safe for its occupants. The frame is not something that the construction crew just throws together, either. It is planned in advance, and the architect formulates the right shape and design for it to match the home that it will be supporting. Everything about the frame, construction, and design is intentional, and we discovered that we should have that same emphasis in our marriage. The more we worked together, the more we learned to play to each other's strengths. Doug is completely different from me, which makes our business great. We improved our communication through counseling and developed mutual respect for each other, and now, we support and encourage each other. I can't think of a better investment that we could have made for our marriage than investing in each other and improving the way that we communicate with one another. We wanted to use the best construction materials to become the best husband-wife team we could be and have the strongest framework possible to bear the weight that any marriage would experience. I encourage you to do the same to shore up the strength of your union with your partner.

KEYS TO HELP YOU FLIP YOUR MARRIAGE

- Effective communication is key in a marriage because it will help you deal with relationship challenges.

- When each partner contributes to the strength of the relationship, it will stand tall despite obstacles.

- Identify how your individual strengths can compensate for and counteract your partner's weaknesses and vice versa.

- A strong frame takes time and effort and cannot be built without hard work, teamwork, and consistency.

- Embrace Godly counseling and mentorship because it can help you create the marriage that you desire.

Chapter 5
Weathering the Bad Times... Your Roof!

Every house needs a roof to protect the structure and everything within the home. If you think about it, you would never buy a home if the roof had visible holes in it. In fact, when we are flipping a home, one of the things that we look at first is the condition of the roof because that can be one of the most expensive parts of a flip. Sure, you can patch up a leaky roof or replace it entirely, but you are much better off if you can find a place that has a roof that is in great condition so that you can put your efforts somewhere else. That is the same principle as marriage. After you get a strong foundation and set up the framing of the home, you need to get a roof overhead to protect you from the elements – literally and figuratively.

The sooner a couple building together can get this roof up, the better off you're going to be. One of the tough parts about marriage is that you've got to keep protecting yourself and your partner from the same things, time and time again. The roof or your head, in a spiritual sense, is the part closest to God. The roof protects the house, and it's the highest point of the structure, and so is your head. I feel like I'm at a point in my life where I'm healing. Healing from childhood trauma, healing from relationships with flawed friends or family, and healing within my own relationship. I love hard, have crazy loyalty for others I love, and by default, I will cut you off long-term too. I had to come to a realization that everyone isn't going to react or treat you the way you would treat yourself and others. In our business together, Doug wants to make sure I don't get pushed over and that I stand strong. I'm naturally an alpha female, yet he knows my heart is so good and trusting.

There is something in my experience about a successful man who protects his wife and his household. That is just a huge turn-on to me, and for the majority of our marriage, I felt that Doug had done a great job with that. Yes, he is a social butterfly, and he is the life of the party, but for the most part, I felt safe being married to him and with him as the protector of our home. For me, feeling protected is at the top of my list with Doug. There have been a few deep situations where I didn't feel like he protected my feelings or the sanctity of our marriage. I mentioned before the attention that his life, or should I say our lives, attracts. There's always someone lurking around trying to get a piece of what you have. People are really attracted to people they think are successful. They want to be in their aura and get connected to them. You really have to watch out for people, especially some of these females who think that they can replace you if they can find a way to sneak their way under your roof and into your life. Females are always messaging him via social media, asking to be a mentee. While some of those requests are legitimate, that is the oldest trick in the book, in my opinion. There is one female in particular that he met for lunch. Now, he already knew that I did not play the radio about people getting too close to him or in our space, and he knew better than to do what he did. I found out using my detective skills because he thought he was so slick. I can laugh now, but I was pissed at the time. Doug says I really should've been a detective. Anyway, they went to lunch to discuss his book and the real estate business. There were a few problems with that. I wasn't there. I didn't know about it; he acted like it wasn't a big deal. Now, however innocent the conversation might have been between them, he forgot that his main jobs were to protect the covering of our home and make sure that I, as his wife, was comfortable. If he needed to meet with her for business, he should have included me so that everything would have been handled professionally and respectfully. Yeah, he was busted, and as I already said, I was pissed!

I ended up speaking to the female on the phone. Yeah, I got her number, and it was all innocent. She actually thought I was going to be there, especially since Doug and I are always together. I still think that she should have requested me to be there when he showed up alone or rescheduled the meeting, but they went ahead and had lunch and talked business. I don't think that Doug initially understood the magnitude of what he did. While I knew he was working to be a different guy as a married man, I also knew that the street hustler who loved women and attention was always lurking beneath the surface. My trust was impacted because I felt that he was sneaking behind my back to see her without my knowledge. The roof for sure had a leak, and our structure/marriage was compromised.

As a result of this situation, we agreed moving forward that I would be invited to any business or mentoring lunches that involved females. He knew what was good for him, and rather than deal with the consequences of another poor decision around women, business, and mentorship, he saw things my way. I'm definitely not the one to test! Social media can lead some people down a dark tunnel. They see you online and think that they know you. They want to be connected to you, and for some people, that attention is too much of a lure for them to resist. They fall prey to bad decisions connected to their need to be wanted and valued by those who are not inside their marriage. I think that Doug learned that it's important to keep things professional so that the other person doesn't get the wrong idea. This situation could have been a real deal breaker because Doug didn't protect our structure.

I will take my "L" on this one because I knew better than to take a meeting without my wife being there with me. As I said before, she had been functioning as my secretary for years. She knew everywhere I was going to be, but this time, I kept the meeting off the books. Now, I have to say that although the lady was a beautiful woman, we did discuss business at the table. She really wanted my mentorship, and she wanted to discuss business with me. I get that all the time. That is just something that I have to deal with because I am a successful entrepreneur. People naturally want to be attached to me, and they want me to teach them what I do so that they can be successful. Something felt off for sure when we got to the restaurant, but I played it cool and stuck to the script the best that I could. Have you ever been somewhere you knew you weren't supposed to be, and you just couldn't get comfortable because you spent the majority of your time looking over your shoulder? That was me for sure. Nothing seemed to go right. I couldn't even enjoy my meal because I was worried that Atiya would call me, or somehow, she would just pop up at the restaurant as if she had a GPS tracker on my car. Again, the meeting was solely business-oriented, but I knew deep down inside that I should have informed Atiya about this meeting. Needless to say, that experience was nothing like our usual meetings with people when we are together.

I still remember the conversation later on when she shared with me that she had contacted the woman and asked her some pointed questions. I couldn't even get angry. In fact, I was more in shock than anything because I never expected it to go to that level. She was furious. I know that she will tell people that I "cuss" all the time. She is such a refined woman with an accent who always seems to say the right thing in the kindest way possible. That is who she is 99% of the time, but in this particular incident, that 1% remaining time was hell on Earth.

Atiya gave it to me in more ways than one. She let me have it, and there was nothing that I could do but sit there and take it. I knew I messed a good thing up. I knew it when I didn't tell her about the lunch and hadn't made sure that she could be there. What was I thinking? That is not how we do business, and now the person I was supposed to be protecting and including in every aspect of my life was furious with me about my lapse in judgment. She kept telling me about her loss of trust in me. She told me that she wasn't sure what I was capable of if I was willing to be so sneaky as to take a meeting with a female client for lunch and keep it from her. Was it worth it? Hell no! In fact, I regret the day that I did that because not only did I damage a potential business relationship with a female client because I made her feel like she was causing me to be dishonest with my wife, but also my wife had serious concerns about my judgment and my ability to remain professional with female clients.

Changes were on the way, and if I wanted to keep my marriage intact and heal my wife's broken heart, I needed to do exactly as she asked. I willingly accepted that I had some more maturing to do in terms of my decision-making process. I admitted to her that I failed to be the covering for our marriage to protect her from feeling exactly how she felt at that moment. I had to recommit to my role as her husband and make the changes that she needed to be comfortable. That was the worst and most awkward conversation that I ever had in my life, but I am a better man for it.

When you commit to being married to someone, you are telling that person that you are willing to deny yourself to ensure that they are safe and happy. There will be some safeguards that you will need to establish that you may not think are necessary, but your partner needs those things to be in place. Your job is to put your partner first in marriage and follow Godly principles to protect your home. You have to think with a "we first" mindset in all that you do. There are some people who cannot come into your space because they will threaten the sanctity of your home. Those are minor sacrifices that you will need to make to ensure that your partner feels safe and secure. I missed that part of my assignment in that instance, but I was willing to listen and pivot, so Atiya could feel the protection that she deserved.

Remember, a home is only as good as the roof that it has overhead. Without the right covering, every drop of rain, flake of snow, or bit of debris from above will come in and destroy what you have built, wear away at the walls, and eat away at the foundation. Make sure that the covering of your home is strong. Use the best shingles for your roof. Participating in counseling, hanging with wise married friends, and praying can ensure that you maintain the life that you have built. Don't be afraid to put in the work to create a solid roof over your marriage. In the end, it is totally worth the work!

CHAPTER 5: WEATHERING THE BAD TIMES...YOUR ROOF!

KEYS TO HELP YOU FLIP YOUR MARRIAGE

- You should expect challenges and issues to occur in your marriage. That is part of the human experience.

- Your spiritual covering should be the roof that helps you weather relationship storms.

- If you have allowed things to infiltrate your relationship, be intentional and dedicated to repairing it.

- Be transparent with your partner about their needs in the marriage and do what it takes to make them comfortable.

- You are a team, and what you do and how you interact with others impacts your partner.

Chapter 6

Materials: Show What You are Made Of!

Now that we have the foundation, the frame, and the roof, let's talk about the materials. Choosing the right materials is important for any renovation or new build. In a marriage, choosing the right spouse (someone you are compatible with) is just as important. When you're young, some of the things that mattered then can change once you're older. Will that person be able to change with you or with your relationship? Windows allow you to see in and out of a house. Transparency in a marriage is comparable to those windows. Doug wasn't always transparent; however, with counseling and deep conversations, that has changed. Doug has shared with me that it's hard for men to sometimes be transparent because they can be made to feel like a child. I've learned to communicate with him in a way about transparency that will not make him feel like this. It's all in how you communicate those needs and why transparency is important for you.

The water heater in a typical home may last for 15-20 years, depending on the brand. At some point, it's definitely going to go out and need to be replaced. The water heater symbolizes the energy and affection in your marriage. It can represent the sexual chemistry that you and your partner share. I joke with my friends often, and say, "I'm keeping it spicy." It's also healthy to have "sex" conversations. It's important that I make sure my husband's needs are being met, and he reminds me that we're all good. He says he has no complaints! After over 20 years of being married, some marriages struggle in this area. For me, it's important that I stay in tune with his sexual needs. From what I've seen in some marriages, this area could lead to major issues if it's not addressed. You definitely don't want your husband's attention to start straying somewhere else; therefore, be sure to keep your marriage lit, like the flame for your water heater.

Another important feature of a home is the door, which could symbolize in and out…an entryway, or privacy. Imagine if your home didn't have any doors. Neighbors would be able to see right into your life. Some married couples may be more open to sharing the details of their marriage, whereas others may have a level of discretion. Doug is usually private when it comes to disagreements or major issues we've had in our relationship. I like to confide in people I trust and vent about how I may be feeling. A healthy relationship has a good balance. Keeping people out of your business, for the most part, is best. Too many opinions can cause disruption or lead to more arguments. When we have our occasional disagreement, we don't share the dirty details of our issues with others; we prefer to reconcile any issues internally and keep our doors closed.

When I am working with my contractors on a property that I am rehabbing, the materials are a very important consideration in everything that I am planning to do. I use the best materials in our flips. In fact, I renovate homes to give buyers champagne on a beer budget, so the materials that we use in the project have to match

CHAPTER 6: MATERIALS: SHOW WHAT YOU ARE MADE OF!

the design and the price of a luxuriously finished home. I would never try to use old nails, lumber, and carpet that I took from a previous project unless the materials were the best. It absolutely would not make sense. I want top-of-the-line materials because my clients are willing to pay a premium price for a high-end home that my team and I flip. They have come to expect no less than that from me. I want my customers to see that I value their project so much that I am willing to use the best of the best in their home's construction. My work in this field speaks for itself, and there is no way that I would risk my reputation by picking the cheapest materials I can find for my projects.

In my opinion, the same concept applies to my marriage. Now, when I was in the streets back in Indiana, I really didn't understand the importance of picking the right woman to be my soulmate. Sure, I knew Atiya was an amazing woman, but there is something about understanding that you have a partner and confidante in your mate who will be there with you when things are great or when life throws its challenges your way. I don't want anyone to think that my professional journey was always rosy and easy. In fact, I had a bunch of pitfalls along the way. For a while, business was not booming, and my wife and I had to make sacrifices over the past 25 years to ensure that we stayed afloat and were able to take care of our children.

One thing I can say about the woman I chose to be my wife is that she never once wavered in her support of me. This is why I say building materials in relation to a marriage are so important. When I was in the streets, and money was coming to me very easily, I attracted a totally different crowd, but not one of those women could hold a candle to what my wife brings to my life. I stand on that! She truly understands what people say about being there for each other through thick and thin, sickness and health, until death do us part. There were so many times that she could have chosen to leave and go back to her family in Indiana when we lived in Kentucky; however, her commitment to us has been unflinching, and that is how I know that I chose to build our home – our marriage – with the most durable materials possible. I learned from her that we had to invest in each other to strengthen our foundation and our framework. We are both fully committed to the process of becoming transparent with each other and improving our communication. That investment has caused our marriage and our business ventures to soar. I was probably the one in the marriage who was the most stubborn and was not as willing to change, but once I realized that I could do so much more when I pulled in the same direction with Atiya, instead of choosing to do my own thing, I think I unlocked the secret that makes us a power couple.

Atiya has always been beautiful to me. Have you ever met a person who's beautiful inside and out? Well, that's my wife – my beautiful angel. I remember the first day that I met her when we were much, much younger. After I gave her my number, a month passed, and I didn't hear from her. I would chase her around town. I saw her driving and would get close and miss her. This went on for over a month. I was at the mall one day and saw her as I drove down the aisle in the parking lot. I can remember it as if it were yesterday. She had on a summer dress that was flowing in the wind, and I said to myself, "There she is." I had her then because apparently, her car wouldn't start. I rolled my window down, smiled, and said, "What happened?" The rest is our story, our life, and our history we are making. She is just a 2.0 version of herself now, but back in the day, we used to talk all the time on the phone, and I couldn't wait to get back to her as soon as possible.

CHAPTER 6: MATERIALS: SHOW WHAT YOU ARE MADE OF!

Atiya was 100% Team Doug back then, and even when we were at our worst point, I knew that the same woman was still inside her. The issue in my mind was me, and the only way we were going to get out of some of the ruts that we were in was that we needed a marriage restoration or a makeover. I never wanted to be without her; however, we both knew that some things had to change if we were going to get back to the happy and loving feelings that we used to have. I have an amazing woman by my side. I decided that if she needed me to move differently and try some new materials in our marriage to renovate it, she wasn't asking too much of me.

Doug has done a 180-degree turn in our marriage, and I have to give him credit for his sincere effort to learn me and cater to my needs. There's always going to be room for improvement. Not every man in a marriage is willing to put in the work, but I think he realized that our marriage and our connection to each other needed to be renovated – and it would be worth the investment. No matter how nice the hardwood floors are in your home, at some point, they will need to be refreshed. They might need to be sanded or stained, and once you put in just a little effort, the floors can look as good as new. That same principle applied to the maintenance that we needed to do to restore our connection. I really used to believe that we never would get past a surface level in our marriage because Doug wouldn't communicate with me in the way that I needed. It was as if he was hiding something from me, or he just didn't want to be vulnerable to me, and that drove me crazy. All I wanted him to know was that I was on his side, and if he would just let me in, I would show him that I was the perfect woman destined for him. I am a woman who believes in the power of counseling and seeking expert help when you have a concern or issue, but I thought the conversation with him on that topic was DOA – dead on arrival.

I thought that maybe he just kept me at arm's length because there were just some things that he didn't want me to know, and he felt that if I didn't get too close to him, he wouldn't hurt me. However, once we unlocked the hidden potential that our marriage possessed through expert help and transparency, our connection and our intimacy exploded. It's kind of hard to explain. We were married and had a closeness; however, now we are inseparable. He often tells me that I am more than a wife. He says I feel like family.

We started running on all cylinders, and he learned to teach me the things that he needs from me to keep him happy. I have 25 years in the game, and I am all about continuing to do what is necessary to protect our investment – our marriage. Doug knows that the more that he gives to me and leans into me as his wife, the more he will get what he needs from me. It is a reciprocal relationship, and I feel that he now understands that we make each other happier when we work together.

Doug has always been a passionate man where I am concerned. I never had to worry whether my husband wanted me. He continues to make that crystal clear, and I had to become vulnerable enough when times were not great to invest in renovating our marriage. I knew that I was making a much better investment in renovating a broken or damaged marriage than throwing it away when the hard times hit. I felt that at the core of us was a connection between two people who loved each other deeply. We just needed more tools in our toolbelt to help us deal with rough patches, such as disagreements and issues in our communication. Our intimacy never faltered in our marriage because I knew that I was still as fine as I was when he fell in love with me. He still looked at me with those same playful bedroom eyes. All I had to do was figure out how to continue igniting the passionate furnace in our marriage, and our natural chemistry would do the rest of the work. The magic was happening in the bedroom, but sometimes not to the level that it could be due to being depleted emotionally or mentally. It's natural if you have communication issues or are just angry at one another. Who feels like jumping right into the bed and pleasing your man? Well, my grandmother would always tell me not to go to bed angry. I'm not going to lie, that was hard. It took a level of maturity on my part to break that pattern and silence. I had the silent treatment down to perfection. Do not play with me.

When you find that your connection with your partner is off, and you want to get back to the loving and committed feelings that you used to have, it is time to try a different approach. Maybe your marriage needs some renovations, such as counseling, like we tried in our marriage. Your marriage is one of the best investments that you will ever make, especially when you are Divinely aligned with the person who will help you grow and evolve. Just because you recognize that you need a different approach does not mean your partner will initially be excited about the work that you need to do. It took Doug a while before he valued the tools that we used to restore and enhance our marriage. Once he was on board, our connection soared. Find the balance and connection in your relationship. Invest in each other and commit to doing the things that will restore your union. Just like you don't want cheap materials used in your dream home, use all the best resources around you to give your marriage the best opportunity to thrive.

KEYS TO HELP YOU FLIP YOUR MARRIAGE

- Your marriage will reveal the work that you have done to grow with your partner.

- Be willing to grow and evolve in your marriage when you are challenged, even if that includes counseling.

- Be transparent with your partner about your needs and be willing to listen to their needs.

- Remain balanced in your communication with your partner and your individual roles and responsibilities.

- Keep others outside your home from knowing your business.

Chapter 7
Wiring...What kind of energy is brought into the marriage?

House electrical wiring is a process of connecting different accessories for the distribution of electrical energy. The most important part about wiring as it pertains to marriage is the distribution of energy, similar to the exchange of love between a husband and wife. This connection is so important in a successful marriage because it impacts how well partners relate to each other, which determines the marriage's ability to withstand the inevitable storms and challenges that it will experience. Without the proper wiring, there is no connection between you and your spouse, and without a strong connection, it is hard for a marriage to thrive.

Wiring in a house is the connection between the both of you. The connection is important to keep everything in the relationship and house operating. I remember years ago when I first started teaching. One of my students' parents was going through a divorce. I usually had long conversations with the mom, and on this particular day, I asked about her marriage and why divorce. She said they grew apart and didn't have anything in common. That was over 25 years ago, and it stuck with me. I would never want to get to the point in my relationship where Doug and I do not have anything in common. We share a lot of things in common that we enjoy, but there are things that I don't like. I try to meet him halfway by still partaking in some of those activities. I like hiking and the outdoors. That's not usually Doug's cup of tea; however, he will go and try new things.

When I think about all the people I know who are either divorced or unable to find their soulmate, I can't help but think about the importance of a strong connection. That student's parent, who told me that she and her husband grew apart and didn't have anything in common, never left my mind. I wondered how they arrived at that point. I am sure that at some point they felt that they were wired together correctly, especially when they were willing to walk down the aisle and pledge their undying love to one another. They must have had sexual chemistry in order to produce a family, but somehow things went awry. Every time I thought about her, I thought about the strength of the wiring between Doug and me. The saying that *opposites attract* could not be more true than when you think of us. I love what is different about him from me. In fact, I don't think that I would want to be married to myself. I am sure that I would get on my nerves, but that man loves me to my core. I love what he brings to the table, and I feel that we make each other better because we are different in many areas. We challenge each other in different ways. We know how to push each other's buttons in a healthy and constructive way.

Doug still looks at me 25-plus years later the same way that he looked at me when we met back in Indianapolis. As a woman and a wife, it is important that your partner is sexually attracted to you. You need to feel that you turn him on and that you are the spark that lights up his life. My husband lets me know in his words and definitely in the way that he touches me that he loves and wants me. Even as we have taken steps to renovate and restore our marriage over the years, I give him credit for making me feel that he needs to remain connected to me. In those moments when life and marriage have been hard, I always have known that my husband and I have electricity between us. There are some things that you can tweak and fix easily, but if you have no connection to your partner and you are not attracted to each other, you face a significant challenge.

We do things now to keep our marriage fresh and ensure that our wiring remains healthy. We still love to go on date nights. I still dress up for him and do things to turn him on. He knows my favorite restaurants. We still go on vacation together, and we do things to push each other's boundaries to stimulate our growth individually and as a couple. Doug always ensures he looks good no matter where he is going. If you know that man, you know that he is always sharp. He makes sure that he doesn't let himself go because he cares how he presents himself and how he represents us when he is away from me. Doug also is a gentleman, and he treats me the same way that he did when he met me. Doug still showers me with love and always praises me publicly. We have discovered new ways to stay connected in order to ignite the passion within our marriage. What made that possible was our willingness to admit that the voltage between us was not as strong as it was previously and our commitment to do whatever we needed to do to make it better. That is a mature approach that I am not sure that every couple is prepared to take; however, I can say with certainty that is what strengthened our marriage during its rocky points.

When I decide to take on a house flip, one of the things that worries me the most is if the wiring of the home is properly installed. That is one thing that you can't skimp on, no matter how much you want to save money. The wiring of a home is like its veins and arteries. Nothing that a homeowner needs will work if there is a shortage in the wiring. I have seen some flips where a contractor before me didn't ground something properly or didn't follow codes when the home was built. It has cost me thousands of dollars to rewire the whole home, so it can pass inspection. The wiring is what brings electricity to the entire home, and it is one of the most important parts of a flip. As I got more experience as a husband, I realized how important the wiring between Atiya and me really was. Yeah, I originally was not worried about that because I knew we had a connection. She was fine, and I was handsome. We had a natural connection. The wiring between us was on fire when we first got together. However, one thing that I didn't think that I would need to do as we got older was to check the connections regularly and do maintenance if I saw that something was not going right. If the sparks in our marriage were not flying like they used to, or if I noticed that our connection was not right, I just ignored it. I buried my head in the sand and focused more on my work.

There have been times in our marriage when it seemed like one or both of us tripped the breaker, and the power completely went out. However, I lacked the skills to diagnose the issue and check the breaker box. I think that sometimes people think that we are just born with the skills to be excellent husbands and wives. That can happen as people get older because our needs and preferences change. You cannot stay stagnant in the way that you approach your spouse because you will not grow with them. I learned that the hard way. We were getting more mature. We were parents, and what Atiya valued in her 20s was not always what she cherished in her 40s. That transition in terms of needs and wants that is natural for women to undergo is something that many men do not understand.

CHAPTER 7: WIRING...WHAT KIND OF ENERGY IS BROUGHT INTO THE MARRIAGE?

Some people think that we just come out of the womb knowing what to do to please our partners in ways that are not sexual. Now just so we are clear, I always knew how to take care of my wife's needs in that way. There were no problems there, but that was not the issue that we were having. I had to learn that I needed to check our connection much more often than I was doing. She wanted more from me than for her to be an object I felt was beautiful and desirable. She wanted me to get to know her on a deeper level and understand what made her happy. That was something that took a lot more work because it was a different kind of work than what I was used to doing. At first, I was like a fish out of water. It was like taking a roofer and telling him that you needed him to be a plumber. He could make the change, but he would need training and time. That was me when I realized that I had to learn to love my wife differently as we got older. Fortunately, I was committed to the process and wanted to know how to reignite the spark between us.

When I am on a construction site and I think that there is a problem with the electrical output in an outlet, I get a voltage meter. It measures the voltage that is coming from a source on a scale, and those readings let me know if the outlet is functioning normally, or if there is low or no voltage. When we realize that there is a voltage problem, it is time for my electrical contractor to come in and address the issue. I draw a parallel to my experience in counseling. I know we talked about it before, but one of the tools I gained from that experience was the ability to examine the electricity in our marriage. Maybe my wife and I were wired differently, and we needed to find new ways to connect with each other. Perhaps our experiences in our childhood created complex wiring structures in our brains, and we could not see the impact of our choices and the ways that we expressed or did not express love toward each other.

My advice to any married couple or people in a relationship is to check your wiring constantly. Don't assume that what you always have done will always work. People change, and so do their needs. You must be willing to check the voltage of your relationship and go back to the drawing board to take a different approach if your partner does not seem as connected to you as they used to be. It is much easier to do routine maintenance on the electrical system of your relationship than it is for you to start all over again and completely reinstall the electrical system in a new relationship. Know your partner and stay in touch with their needs. If you are willing to pivot if things are not going the way that you know they should go, you will be able to maintain a strong connection with your mate. You can get those sparks flying again if you are willing to put in the work.

KEYS TO HELP YOU FLIP YOUR MARRIAGE

- The energy that you bring to the marriage will impact how your partner connects with you.

- Keep things fresh in your relationship and be willing to try new things to please your spouse.

- Ensure that your partner feels loved and wanted by the things you say to them and do for them.

- Don't skimp on your efforts to make a good impression on your partner.

- Take the temperature of your marriage regularly, and if things are not going as they should, make a pivot.

Chapter 8
Systems in place!

All homes have essential systems in place. Those systems include plumbing, water, heating and air, electrical, locks, and security. These are the systems and processes that make a house function. Your marriage will involve multiple systems too. Some of those systems in your marriage entail who does what in the household. We live a very non-traditional lifestyle at home. Of course, I would love for Doug to always take the trash out. He gets away with not doing it when our sons are home. Our oldest son just recently moved out, and our youngest is a senior in college. I've always tried to set a great example for our sons of what a wife and mother should resemble. My wish is that when they choose a partner, she shares the same passions, is loyal, is trustworthy, and loves them as I do.

There are days when Doug may not have time to take the trash out, so I will take it out. I have this thing about no dishes being left in the sink overnight, but if I happen to fall asleep, he loads the dishwasher. Financially, there were times when I had to pick up more of the household bills because early on, he wasn't as established. Summer football camps, cooking on a griddle in the hotel, or cashing in coins was not unheard of. We ensured we showed up for one another and that our sons were not affected. Systems in a house work together, and I feel like the systems or roles we've established work. We're many years away from when we struggled financially; however, being able to budget is still engraved.

I married a true angel on Earth, and I can say that without exaggerating. I really believe that there is one person who was built just for us, and Atiya is that woman for me. Every time I look at my children, I think about how important she has been in their development. Hell, she has been important in my development. Our oldest son, Drezyn, is a mechanical engineer, and that alone is something that just makes me smile every time I say it. Our youngest son, Dealo, is studying communications in college and will graduate this year. My oldest son, Dasmond, is married with one child and is doing a great job holding his household down. My relationship with my son, Douglas III, has been strained over the years; however, I still learn life lessons from my children. Each one has different parts of me that I'm proud of. I was a true street hustler when Atiya met me, and yet, she has been able to turn me into a successful entrepreneur who can move in any group of people. Our second oldest child together is about to graduate from college, and we have been able to pay for their tuition and even their cars in cash without getting into debt. To me, that shows the power of our union and the impact of marrying the right person.

While we have amazing children together, one thing that I love about Atiya is that she shows the same love to my children from previous relationships. In total, I have five children – all boys. Unfortunately, as noted in an earlier chapter, one of my sons passed away, but Atiya loved all of them equally. She came into my three children's lives when they were toddlers and elementary age, but she loved them, and then she gave me two more sons later in our relationship. I am truly blessed that I married someone who supports me personally and professionally, so I can be the man I have been destined to be.

One thing that people always ask me about is what changed in my mind to try to convince my wife to go and get her real estate license when she had such a successful career as an educator. I mean, my wife had a Ph.D., and she was killing the game in school, but I kept working on her to come and join me. People can't understand why I would want to interrupt her workflow to help me flip houses. I think that the answer is quite simple. See, you have to understand that my wife has been my right-hand assistant the whole time. She had been working behind the scenes to help me grow my flipping business. It was only natural in my mind that I ask her to help me in a more official capacity. If she could dominate the game in the field of education, my mind told me that there was nothing that she couldn't do in real estate.

As Atiya stated, we have a non-traditional marriage, but it works for us. She knows who she married and all that comes with me, but I can tell you that she shows me that she loves me and accepts me for who I am. I know that she has a pet peeve about the dishwasher, but I also know that if I just take a few minutes to load the dishwasher, the crisis will be averted. Now, I don't wash dishes by hand, but I know I can at least help out in that manner. I had to learn my wife's love language and figure out what I could do to keep her happy.

I remember one day I was working on an idea for flipping a property, and I realized that I wanted bigger and better things for my business. Yeah, I had celebrity clientele who really were a strong *backbone of my business, but I just really felt like there was another level that I hadn't reached yet. I looked over at my wife. I mean, I really looked at her while she was sitting on the couch, and I thought about it. She was the missing piece in growing my business. She had all the intangibles that I was missing, and if I could convince her to come on board with me in a more official capacity, I knew that we could work as a team and tackle just about anything.*

To understand me, you have to know how I think. By now, you know that I am a street hustler at heart. It is all in me, and I just think on that level, but sometimes, that approach is what you need in this business. I know how people think, especially celebrities, and I realized that my wife has the look and the soft touch to reach them in ways I cannot. I had to put my ego aside and realize that we would be much more effective together than if I just kept working on my business by myself. She is very easy on the eyes, and she has that sweet Southern drawl that I know makes people comfortable. I could just see in my head how my clients would be so much more comfortable with her as their agent, and they probably would spend money on a home because she pitched it to them versus me as the salesman. I saw an angel with her that I didn't have, and I asked her to come on board with me. I knew that we'd have our own roles and parts to play in our business, but she was everything that I wasn't, and I needed her with me.

Those systems that we have in place in our marriage impact our roles in the business. Doug showed me that he wanted me to work with him to help him grow his business in a different way. I was skeptical at first, but because I allow him to be the head of our household, and I trust his vision for us, I was willing to take my real estate test and jump out officially into the business. It was a different feeling when I was working with clients and training people how to flip homes for themselves, but the feeling that I had when I realized that my husband both needed and trusted me to be his partner in business was indescribable. It reminded me of the importance of our roles and our relationship first, which made a successful business relationship so easy.

I also loved that we still found a way to raise our children together and give them the time and attention that they deserved even while we pursued our individual and collective business goals. Doug trusted my approach in making sure that our home ran smoothly and things were done in an orderly and effective manner. He knew that there were just certain things at which I excelled, and the best thing that he could do sometimes was to just let me do it my way. Most women wish their husbands understood that. I never made him feel less than a man or less than the leader of our home because we learned to respect each other for our differences. Sometimes, I would yield to his opinion on a topic, and other times, he would go with my recommendation. There was a clear give and take in our marriage that gave everyone a chance to lead.

If you are in a marriage or are interested in marrying someone, it is important that you determine what your systems need to be to help your union to be successful. Little things can become major if you don't address them in a timely manner. Just like we had to decide how and when the dishes would be washed, you will have things in your relationship that require agreement. You also will need to determine roles in your marriage. Sometimes the husband will need to defer to the wife's wisdom on an issue. It wasn't a fight in our marriage because Doug knew he could trust my judgment. Other times, the husband needs to be the head of the household and lead his family. I could follow Doug because he always has been a hard worker, and if there was one thing that I could count on, it was that he was going to provide for us. You have to marry someone who complements your weaknesses, and Doug and I have found that balance in marriage, which is why we still continue to thrive together 25+ years after we started this amazing union.

> **KEYS TO HELP YOU FLIP YOUR MARRIAGE**
>
> - While falling in love and remaining in love are important, other factors such as financial stability are also essential in a marriage.
>
> - Determine what systems your marriage needs to have to keep your union fresh, and do what works best in your relationship.
>
> - Your relationship will have trials and trauma, and the systems that you have in place will help you deal with those challenges.
>
> - Ensure that your partner knows that you appreciate and respect what they bring to the marriage.
>
> - Address any minor issues that you have in your relationship to prevent them from becoming major problems.

Chapter 9
I'm gonna blow this house down... let us pray!

No one is perfect. I am not perfect, and I didn't marry a perfect man. I told you all I was a detective at heart, and that can definitely be a downfall. I also think that in the world we live in, there will always be people who are not happy for you or your success. They want what they think that you have, and many people are willing to do whatever they can to get a piece of the picture-perfect life that they assume that you have. Unfortunately, sometimes, it can be people close to you. They are watching your every move to find an opening where they can get into your marriage.

I am not going to exonerate my husband for some of the poor decisions that he has made in our marriage. Doug has definitely made decisions in our marriage, as mentioned previously, where I wanted to blow the house down. You can't change a person, but what you can do is pray and ask God to change your heart. I know that may sound strange. That was an area of growth for me because a mean spirit certainly wanted to come out of me a few times in our marriage, and I can assure you that God would not have been pleased with how I was going to handle things. Why am I praying that my heart changes?

Sometimes our vision or perception needs to change. I needed God to change the bitterness in my heart so that I could have clarity.

Over the years, I've been intentional with my prayers. Faith, God, and praying have always been very important to us. I would pray for God to change my heart or show me signs if Doug and I weren't meant to be together. I never saw signs; however, I added a special prayer. I prayed and still do for God to protect our household and marriage, keep us in a bubble, protect us from anyone who means us harm, continue to lead us in the right direction, and help us grow together. I pray for God to allow us to serve as a model to other couples and as a model for our children and family. We pray together on our knees, and we thank God continuously for all of our blessings now and the ones to come. I pray for patience, too, because it's not always easy working with your spouse!

Now, I don't want to act as if praying for my husband has always fixed things quickly. It took me a long time to get to this level of spiritual maturity, and my gangsta has been tested quite a few times along the way. There have been times that I had to look at God and ask, "What are you waiting for?" When you are invested in your marriage, and you want the absolute best for your partner, there are going to be times that you must pray more than once for what you want. I can't tell you how often I stayed on my knees in prayer for Doug. I just wanted God to help him to see things my way, so we could move forward in our relationship. If God would just come in like a brisk wind and change all the things that I wanted him to do differently, I just knew that we would have the perfect marriage, and I would be the perfect wife.

I can say honestly that my prayers were selfish sometimes because I wanted God to fix him, but I didn't see the need for me to change.

CHAPTER 9: I'M GONNA BLOW THIS HOUSE DOWN...LET US PRAY!

My thoughts were all outwards because I felt that he was the problem. There were things that I have shared that he did that drove me crazy, but I also needed to adjust how I thought about marriage. God began to answer my prayers for my husband, but His answers didn't always come in the way that I anticipated. When God started revealing to me things that I also needed to change and address, things got a little uncomfortable for me. I knew that He was working on Doug because I started to see some changes in how he was moving in our marriage. I thanked God for that growth, but I struggled with the things that God wanted to see me do to become a better wife. Questions that I had to consider included: Did I make him feel like the head and covering of our home at all times? Were there times when I was so busy with what I had going on professionally and personally that I put my husband on the back burner?

Being a mother, a wife, a professional, and an entrepreneur means that you must wear different hats at the same time. I don't think that you really can be prepared for how well you need to balance your time and energy until you are in the thick of being married. I knew I was a great mother to our children, including Doug's kids from before we got married. I had that part on lock. I knew that I was an excellent educator. My test scores and my feedback from my administrators told me that. Once I transitioned out of the classroom into a leadership role, my time was even more limited. I knew that I was supporting my husband as an entrepreneur. He regularly included me in his business and asked me to get my real estate license because he knew how valuable I was to our growth. I also knew that I took care of him in the bedroom. However, something was missing in our relationship that contributed to some of the decisions that he was initiating, and I needed God to reveal to me what He wanted me to do differently to strengthen and restore my relationship with my husband.

They say that cats have nine lives, but I can assure you that I think I have the cats beat out for that record. It took me a long time to get myself together on a regular basis. I mean, my heart was in the right place 99% of the time, but that 1% of the time that my attention was not where it needed to be could have cost me everything. I just have a natural air about me that makes people want to get close to me. Some people call it my charisma, but whatever it is, it works well in business to help me get clients and close deals, but it can become problematic when I don't know how to turn it off. I have to give my wife credit for being as longsuffering with me as she has been. I am sure that other women would have left their husbands a long time ago, but I got a good one for sure. God really knew what He was doing when he matched us together.

That last time that I got myself in hot water with my wife, I knew that I had to do something different. I kept thinking about the fact that we built an entire life together in business and with our children, and I was throwing away my chance at happiness. I was committing unforced errors in my marriage, and I really had no reason to make them. What did I have to complain about with my wife? She always kept herself up, no matter where we were going or what she was doing. She never tried to upstage me or take the limelight away from me. I actually didn't realize how important that was until I almost lost her.

It is crazy to think about the warning signals that you can miss when you are so into yourself and what you are doing that you close your eyes to what is going on around you. Now that I think about it, the warning signs of women who were far too interested in me as a person, and in being in my orbit, were all there. I started to lose my way because the fame and success professionally were clouding my judgment. I was so focused on winning the daily real estate battles to make money and get new clients that I was in danger of losing the war for my family.

I will never forget the day that my wife came to me, and I could tell in her eyes that she had had enough. It wasn't that I had been unfaithful to her, but it was the boundaries that she felt I crossed numerous times. She didn't think that I took my role seriously as the protector of our home, and either I was going to make the changes that she needed or she was going to leave me. The idea of her not being in my life was not even a possibility to me, and something told me that I needed to listen to her this time. She laid out to me all the things that I had been doing to hurt her. She told me about the boundaries that I didn't have and the people I let infiltrate our marriage. I couldn't believe how bad I had let things get. Moreover, I know that she had been praying for me and for our marriage, and there was no way I could ignore what she was saying to me.

It was at that moment, when the fate of my marriage was at stake, that I decided that I had to make a decision. I needed to develop boundaries in my personal and professional life that would communicate to my wife that I loved and respected her. She had turned to prayer to ask God for help to save our marriage, and that was the only thing that I could think of as well that would help us. At that moment, it didn't matter that one of us grew up as a Muslim and the other grew up as a Christian. All that mattered was that the fate of my marriage to my best friend was in its worst shape, and we had to do something together to save it. You can get really desperate when you are down to your last, and your creativity will soar. As we sat there on our knees together, praying for our marriage, we decided that what we had was worth saving, and I decided that I had to make some changes and some sacrifices.

Doug and I learned through our marital issues and trials that we either could blow our house down and try to start our lives over with other people, or we could lean in to each other and love each other the way that we should. I knew I loved Doug with all my heart, but I needed him to respect me when I was in front of him and when I was away from him. I wanted God to fix all the things that I felt were wrong with him, but I also had to be prepared for the changes that God wanted from me to help me to be a better wife to him.

Change is not always going to be the way you want it to be, but if you are committed to loving your partner and doing things in a Godly way, you can learn and grow together. We decided that what we had was worth saving. I am glad that I waited on God to convince Doug of the things that he needed to change to love me properly, and I was willing to accept and forgive him when he did the things that God led him to do to strengthen our marriage. Moving together required equal sacrifice from us, but the results of our decision to follow God's lead in our relationship have been amazing.

KEYS TO HELP YOU FLIP YOUR MARRIAGE

- Stay plugged in spiritually in your marriage because the enemy will try to destroy your relationship.

- You cannot force change on your partner; people will change when they are inspired to make different choices.

- Change in marriage takes time, and you need to be willing to allow God to do His work.

- When God gives you another chance to live your life in accordance with His will, make the changes.

- Respect is a two-way street, and once you establish it in your relationship, your marriage will thrive.

Chapter 10

We Nailed it!

Did we nail it in the beginning? Of course not, because it takes years to be a skilled builder or flipper—and the same is true with a relationship. It doesn't matter the size of the house you build or flip. You have to maintain it! Don't take for granted that what you put into the house will never quit on you. It doesn't matter how expensive the dishwasher is. It will stop at some point if it is not maintained. That flashy paint color you had to have will chip. The roof that you put on the home will start to fade and leak 10-15 years after you install it, and you can't afford to lay the foundation and never check to make sure that runoff from the gutters isn't eroding the soil from around your house.

Always be in tune with your marriage's needs. Doug was building a million-dollar home in Fayette County. He had the foundation and frame up, but he ended up having to just sell it and walk away. There were issues presented that made it difficult to move forward, just like some marriages exist only for a season. I know we often hear that cliché, but it's true. A person can be in your life for a season, a reason, or even a lifetime. All marriages aren't meant to last, regardless of the work you put in. Knowing when to walk away can be difficult, and I suggest praying about it first. I'm so glad that Doug and I are in love. We not only love each other but truly enjoy being with one another. Doug is my best friend. He is the funniest man I have ever met, and I know that God made him especially for me. I can't imagine my life without him. Many people can't say that they married their best friend, but I can say that without a shadow of a doubt.

I like to use the analogy of a house that deteriorates over the years. The deterioration is different depending on if you completed any renovations over the years. Once the renovations are finished, your house feels new again. We surely had some bumpy patches in our marriage, as do most relationships, but we also learned how to love each other in the ways that we preferred. With all our might, we dug our heels in as deep as we could to work as a unit. There are times in our marriage now that Doug feels like my high school sweetheart. I think he understands me and invests time and energy into dating me all over again. We put the effort into learning each other's needs and growing together, so we could prevent the issues that plagued our relationship before we developed the tools to move in harmony. In a marriage, once you make it to the other side of the renovations or revival of the relationship, it's so much better.

I really had to go back and remember some of the traumatic events that I experienced in our marriage when we were writing this book because we are so far on the other side of life together. I put those things behind us because I prayed for peace, a restored marriage, and unconditional love from my husband. God gave me tenfold what I requested, and my husband and I have moved forward together. At least in our case, our love for one another is deeper and more refined. I like to think that our love has aged and matured

CHAPTER 10: WE NAILED IT!

like fine wine. When we were young, we didn't know what it really meant to be committed to another person until death. There were times that I didn't think that the sacrifice was worth the pain that I endured to make my marriage work, but when Doug and I started working together, I finally understood just how amazing our union really was. The beauty that sometimes comes out of pain can be euphoric. I am living in that euphoria right now because we are experiencing the things at this juncture of our lives that I prayed about when the storms in our marriage almost destroyed us. For us, that maintenance meant that we solicited the support of counseling and turned our marriage over to God. We knew that we didn't have the tools to maintain our relationship in a way that would sustain it, so we brought in experts to help us.

My wife and I found a way to beat the odds and nail this beautifully complex thing we call marriage. We consider you family now because we have been transparent with you about our ups and downs in marriage. We didn't hold anything back from you because we wanted you to see that sometimes, you have to be honest with yourself and your partner when you mess up. You can't pretend that your actions do not impact the one you love, especially when you know that you should have been moving differently. I didn't know what I was getting myself into when I asked my wife to marry me. All I knew was that I loved her with all my heart and was willing to do what I thought she needed to make her happy. I was pleased that I did a successful flip and built a life with her. No one told me I had to perform regular maintenance on the marriage after we said, "I do." That is where I had to learn some of the hardest lessons in marriage.

The other thing about marriage is that when you mess up and offend your partner, they aren't going anywhere like a person does if they are just your boyfriend or girlfriend. You have to stay in the mess that you created and find a way to work on what you did until it can be addressed and fixed. That was one of the hardest lessons that I had to learn. My wife was my forever person, which meant that when I made her angry with the choices I made, she was right there every day as a reminder that I had to fix it and make things right. I couldn't go to my place, and she couldn't go to her place. We had a life together with children, so in those moments that were dark and painful between us, I learned the importance of maintaining and fixing things when they needed attention.

Working diligently on my marriage really shouldn't have been such a foreign concept to me when you think about what I do for a living. There is no way that I would flip a house and not check out all of the elements that are important, like the foundation, walls, roof, and systems in the home. If there is an issue with them, I always repair and replace things. The crazy part is that some of the flips that I have done with houses are even more valuable and beautiful than new construction projects. With my creativity, I can take a broken home that is in disrepair, and I can rehab it to the point that it is priceless to one of my clients. They are in awe of the choices that I make when I flip a home, and I realized that I needed to take a similar approach to my marriage.

My marriage was no different because it was in disrepair because of some of the choices that I made. I didn't repaint the walls when the paint began to fade. I didn't replace the roof when the shingles began to crack and fall off. I didn't provide support to the foundation when the house began to settle, the home became unstable, and the walls began to crack. I didn't think that I needed to do that kind of work for my marriage. Once God got my attention through the prayers of my wife and the guidance of our counselor, I began to apply the same principles of flipping a home into its peak condition to my relationship with Atiya.

Now don't get me wrong. I have always showered my wife with gifts and affection, which are my love languages. She has always come first in my eyes, and no other woman could even compare. However, she needed more from me. People have always commented on our love and the type of relationship we have. They say it's something to be admired. But now, I pour myself into my marriage with even greater intention – like I would if I were doing a flipping project or conducting a house search for a celebrity client – and that has been the best investment that I ever could have made. I encourage each of you to think about what matters most to you.

I really want you to focus on what would bring you the most happiness and joy in your life. Would running around town and getting the love and affection of others bring you more joy than the admiration of the person God gave to you? Is it a better deal for you to invest outside your home or work to improve the marriage that you asked God to give you? Trust me when I tell you that there is no better investment than investing in the health of your marriage. If Atiya and I can do it, so can you. I don't claim to be the smartest guy out there, but I know a good deal when I see it. I can tell you without even blinking that the best deal I ever made in my life was to give my marriage to God, ask for and seek the forgiveness of my wife, and invest all of myself into developing a relationship with her that is a shining example of love for others to follow. If you follow our lead, and follow God's blueprint, you too can "nail" your relationship and have the most amazing relationship possible.

KEYS TO HELP YOU FLIP YOUR MARRIAGE

- Remain in tune with your partner's needs and do what is necessary to grow together.

- Your partner should be your best friend, so treat them as you want to be treated.

- Any relationship can deteriorate over time, so it is up to you to find ways to strengthen and revive it.

- When God grants you restoration in your relationship, move forward in love together.

- Keep things fresh and treat your partner like your boyfriend or girlfriend, no matter how long you have been together.

Epilogue

Flipping what we love, one house at a time! The evolution of Bricks and Blondie: We love hard and play hard. We make money together, and some may say that money is the root of all evil. Money can also be the root of happiness. The life that we've been afforded to live and share would not be possible without money. On the flip side, there is nothing worse than having money, but your relationship is falling apart. Building a home and business together that has a foundation of love is a priority for us. It's something we are not willing to give up! It wasn't easy by any stretch of the imagination. Our journey was filled with pitfalls, temptations, and challenges. At the end of the day, we decided that what we built together and what we could create as a unit was completely worth it.

Money has never defined us; however, we do love walking away from the closing table together. We have that and more in our relationship as we have grown and matured together, but our journey here was a very interesting and, at times, messy process. We have shared some of our most transparent and painful moments in this book in the hopes that you will be inspired by our story to flip your relationship, so you and your partner can operate at your peak performance. Don't negate the importance of checking in with each other and performing routine maintenance in your relationship, so it can operate at its best. Your union and your potential together are worth the effort that you will put into your marriage.

Now that we have that out of the way, let's get back to the *bag*, or should we say the fun stuff – the rollercoaster ride! They say diamonds are a girl's best friend, until she flips that first house. In our case, I have my diamonds and our flips too!

EPILOGUE

MAJOR KEYS 🔑 ~ JOURNAL PAGE

MAJOR KEYS 🔑 ~ JOURNAL PAGE

MAJOR KEYS ~ JOURNAL PAGE

MAJOR KEYS 🔑 ~ JOURNAL PAGE

EPILOGUE

MAJOR KEYS 🔑 ~ JOURNAL PAGE

MAJOR KEYS ~ JOURNAL PAGE

EPILOGUE

MAJOR KEYS ~ JOURNAL PAGE

MAJOR KEYS ~ JOURNAL PAGE

~Couples Connection~

Something I've learned about you in the past year

_____
_____
_____
_____
_____
_____
_____

Something I've learned about you in the past year

_____
_____
_____
_____
_____
_____
_____

Something I appreciate about you

_____

_____

_____

_____

_____

_____

_____

Something I appreciate about you

_____

_____

_____

_____

_____

_____

_____

EPILOGUE

FAVORITE MARRIAGE QUOTES

"A happy marriage is a long conversation which always seems too short."
—André Maurois

"Happy is the man who finds a true friend, and far happier is he who finds that true friend in his wife."
—Franz Schubert

"Sensual pleasures have the fleeting brilliance of a comet; a happy marriage has the tranquility of a lovely sunset."
—Ann Landers

"A simple 'I love you' means more than money."
—Frank Sinatra

"There is no more lovely, friendly, and charming relationship, communion or company than a good marriage."
—Martin Luther

"Being someone's first love may be great, but to be their last is beyond perfect."
—Anonymous

"The greatest marriages are built on teamwork. A mutual respect, a healthy dose of admiration, and a never-ending portion of love and grace."
—Fawn Weaver

OUR WEDDING DAY~JULY 3, 1999

PLACE: LEXINGTON, KENTUCKY

BRIDE'S SONG: *HERE AND NOW* BY LUTHER VANDROSS

FIRST DANCE: *HAPPILY EVER AFTER* BY CASE

EPILOGUE

To my love....

You are my first love, my last love, and my everything.

About The Authors

Douglas Parson Jr. (Bricks/Doug The Plug)

As a top Celebrity realtor in the Atlanta area for over 20 years, Douglas has dominated the business by specializing in luxury estates, foreclosures, short sales, new construction etc. He has sold millions of dollars in the Georgia market and even other states. Currently living South of Atlanta, GA with his wife of over 25 years, who is also a realtor. From the East side of Indianapolis, he attended John Marshall Jr. High, and then attended Arlington High School. He was known as a hustler, and left Indianapolis in 1996, and changed his life and career path. Now very blessed, he wants to help people by teaching them "The Art of Flipping Bricks" …. flipping houses. His goal is to change the lives of people who never thought they could invest in real estate (hustlers, dancers, minorities, etc.). His book is a #1 best seller on Amazon, available on Walmart.com, Barnes and Noble, Books-A-Million and where most other books are sold. He even has an audio version available on iTunes, Audible, and Amazon Music. The process of flipping homes is broken down into simple easy to follow steps.

Atiya Parson, Ph.D. (Blondie)

Atiya is a born leader with an entrepreneur spirit. She grew up in Indianapolis, and attended a private school called Children's House until high school. She graduated from Broad Ripple High school and then went on to graduate with honors from the University of Kentucky in Lexington. She has worked in the field of education for over 20 plus years. One of her greatest accomplishments in this field was earning her doctorate degree in 2013. Atiya has a passion for teaching and mentoring. Since joining the real estate arena with her husband Doug, she has taken that same approach with her clients. She enjoys flipping/renovating homes and staying abreast of all the real estate trends.

Key takeaways~ don't be afraid to take chances or try something new. You're not stuck! Life is all about learning, self-improvement, and change. Take a leap of faith and follow your dreams. If you don't, they'll just be that...."dreams".

Ready and eager to take on this new challenge!

www.ingramcontent.com/pod-product-compliance
Lightning Source LLC
Chambersburg PA
CBHW071222160426
43196CB00012B/2378